HUNGRY FOR MORE

HUNGRY FOR MORE

Story and Science to Inspire Weight Loss from the Inside Out

By Adrienne Youdim, M.D.

ISBN: 978-0-578-87563-7

TABLE OF CONTENTS

Prologue:
Pandemic 2020

When the quarantine began in the spring of 2020 due to the novel coronavirus, I had already finished 350 pages of what I thought was a first draft of this book and was excited about the prospect of finally completing the manuscript. I thought perhaps the silver lining to a worldwide pandemic was time, space, and the emotional wellspring that allowed for writing. I felt deeply that this was an opportunity to take stock of what was truly important, to realign with my values, and to eliminate what did not serve me.

But there wasn't much time. There wasn't much space. And while my emotions were heightened, they were not available to me as a source of creativity or inspiration.

There was a beauty in all of us being under one roof, but there was also a nervous energy. The kids needed extra hugs and extra reassurance. My 7-year-old took up residence in my bed, sleeping between my husband and me for what seemed to be an indefinite arrangement. There were constant disruptions in my work to make lunch or to sharpen a pencil. The house was busting at the seams with clutter. Notebooks and pencils on the floor, used masks strewn all around the house, piles of shoes at the doorway, and a sink perpetually filled with dishes waiting for me at the close of my workday. My phone dinged repeatedly with an incessant stream of text messages from friends and family unloading anxieties about this virus they felt that I as a physician could relieve. Not to mention the mind-boggling conspiracy theories, the unveiling of social injustice, and the political upheaval which shocked, pained, and enraged me. Sheltering from home took away any semblance of boundaries and personal space and allowed for unprecedented access to me physically and emotionally. It did not feel like I was taking stock. It felt like chaos. And yet I was keenly aware of my privilege. I was not on the front lines, I had the luxury of working from home, I was healthy, I was not isolated, and yet I was unraveling.

Meanwhile, my routines were deteriorating.

My husband, a surgeon, was unable to work from home and expended his creative energy by cooking and baking. Night after night we indulged on decadent dinners and sourdough bread. Lots and lots of bread. At first, I shrugged my shoulders at the scale. As far as I could tell, the entire planet was gaining weight during quarantine. Besides, I ate, slept, and breathed diet and nutrition. I knew how to take off the pounds when I was ready.

But in my indifference, a few pounds became a few more. And then something happened. I started to wrinkle my nose at my reflection in the mirror. I started to feel resentment at the bulge forming around my midsection. Not that I was swooning over myself pre-pandemic, but certainly gone were the days when my self-perception was tied to micro-changes in my girth or the numbers on the scale. I was no longer that child who wished for the genetics of someone slender and tall. I was no longer the teen who scrutinized every inch of my body. There was no guilt or shame, anger, or resentment. I had been at peace with my body *for years*. And then we were quarantined.

I remember thinking, *Really? Have I come back to this, again?*

Meanwhile, I continued to consult with patients, and I was seeing all of this play out on a grand scale. I was witnessing en masse how boredom, listlessness, sadness, loneliness, fear, anxiety, and social isolation were kicking up old wounds and dormant hungers. Given my privilege to talk to patients from my living room in the midst of such trying circumstances, I was reminded that hunger is universal. Hunger for certainty, self-acceptance, belonging, and connection is a universal human experience. Life and circumstance—be it sickness, divorce, abuse, trauma, hardships both big and small—will upend us again and again and again and reveal our hunger. Unfortunately, we are not taught to understand this hunger, nor are we allowed to tolerate it. We are not taught to embrace ourselves in times of need. We are not taught that there is no shame in feeling fear and longing. Rather, we are conditioned to swallow them. We liken our hunger to an affliction, a scarlet letter that inadvertently exposes our humanity. Ironically, all the suppressing and rejecting only magnifies our hunger and the fear that it cannot be satisfied, averting our attention from the invitation that it presents—the invitation to accept our common humanity with understanding and self-compassion.

A longtime patient of mine—we will call him Craig—was seeing me weekly for virtual visits during this time as he needed the extra support in the midst of all this uncertainty. Craig had a childhood history of sexual abuse and abused drugs and alcohol as a young adult. Sobriety transferred his addiction to food, and he struggled with weight cycling for years prior to coming to see me. When we met, the timing seemed right. He had just had his first child. He was in therapy. His home life and work life were stable, and he was entering his 5th year drug and alcohol free.

By the time we transitioned to virtual visits, Craig had already lost 65 pounds—the most weight loss he had ever achieved. He was pleased, and I was too, pleased yet cautious. After over a decade of this work, I knew that no one ever fully arrives. No one loses 65 pounds to the sound of blaring trumpets and confetti, at which point they ride off into the sunset to the sounds of happily ever after. *Arriving* would mean our work is done, and we all know that our work is never really done.

For the first several weeks of the pandemic, Craig continued to do well, surprisingly upbeat despite the uncertainty. And then a few months in, he lost his job. Several weeks later, his mother was diagnosed with cancer. The heartache was just too much to bear and triggered old patterns. The feelings of sadness and loss brought up old traumas that drove him to old habits which he had not engaged in over the years that we had worked together. His first "off-the-wagon" experience, as he put it, was a night of bingeing. He had eaten an entire pizza alone. But he was able to recognize the trigger and bring himself back.

"That's resilience," I said, in response to the shame reflected in his downtrodden eyes.

The next week, Craig skipped his appointment with me. I could only imagine that maybe he was bingeing again, and that shame or disappointment or self-condemnation kept him from coming back. I wished I could tell him that Katie, whom I had just spoken to, was also struggling. So were Marty and James, and yet with an abundance of self-compassion, they had persevered and resumed their course. I wished I could console him that this process of coming to terms with food, to coming to terms with our hunger, is a reckoning, an evolution, a gradual unfolding whereby weaknesses and shortcomings shape and mold us to a more resilient and self-assured place. Everyone faces road bumps at some point. Sometimes the setbacks are so slight that they are perceived by no one but us, and other times they feel insurmountable. But either way, no one evades the process.

I wanted to tell him that I too am struggling but opted against self-disclosure. And so, in the midst of sourdough bread and wine, Craig inspired me to sit at my computer again to write his story, to write my stories, and to write the stories of many that I have collected over the years—the stories that describe what it is that we are truly hungry for.

INTRODUCTION

BY THE TIME PEOPLE come to see me, *a weight loss doc*, they have already tried everything. Keto, intermittent fasting, paleo, low-cal, low-carb, the Blood Type Diet, South Beach, and many *many* more. They have tried commercial weight loss programs like Weight Watchers, Lindora, Nutrisystem, and Jenny Craig to name a few. They have downloaded apps and counted calories, weighed their food on miniature scales and measured them in serving cups and spoons or just with the palm of their hand. They have consumed pink-flavored protein shakes and portion-controlled bags of high-protein peanut butter and cheddar snacks. They have hired trainers and signed up at gyms, and some even recall bouncing up and down in pink leotards and leg warmers to the voice of Richard Simmons from their very own living room. I just barely missed that boat myself. Many have skeptically yet expectantly tried over-the-counter fat blockers and metabolism boosters with the hopes that maybe these tablets might be the long-sought-after answer to their weight loss woes. Some have tried shots, others have been prescribed pills, and still others have had bands and balloons placed around or inside their stomachs or have had their stomachs partially removed for the purpose of weight loss.

Regardless, those who make it into my office, usually, are *not* newbies, and they come asking one question: "What is finally going to work?"

For years I felt pressure to answer that question in an eloquent soundbite. I *was* the doctor after all. I felt the pressure to satisfy timelines, to make assurances and guarantees even though my intuition told me otherwise. I felt responsible to rectify the years of diets, pills, and supplements that had failed them by prescribing other diets and pills and supplements as well. I am all for tools that can help my patients in this journey, and despite a deluge of weight-loss gimmicks, there are evidence-based tools and strategies that are effective in helping people achieve weight loss, many of which I prescribe.

But as my patients often lament, these tools, on their own, do not work.

Nothing works.

Because tools cannot take the place of process. Tools cannot replace the painstaking work, time, practice, patience, perseverance, resilience, deliberation, intention, understanding, self-compassion, and self-awareness necessary to engage and persist in this effort. Tools cannot restore our sense of self, nor can they restore balance to our lives. Tools cannot replace the deep reckoning that uncovers our true *hunger.*

We are hungry, in fact we are *starving,* for belonging, connection, self-love, self-acceptance, patience, approval, presence, equanimity, and autonomy, among so many other hungers, as the following stories will describe. While the flavor may be different, the sentiment is not. We are all hungry to live fulfilled, contented, wholehearted lives. We experience our emotional hunger viscerally, like a gnawing sensation in our gut. Something akin to physiologic hunger. But it is not food we hunger for. Perhaps this is most keenly described by Dr. Edith Eger, author, psychotherapist, and Auschwitz survivor:

We are hungry. We are hungry for approval. We are hungry for attention, for affection, we are hungry for the freedom to embrace life and really know and be our true self.

Disconnection from that which we yearn for leaves a hunger that longs to be filled. That gnawing hunger, when left unattended, is filled by busyness, work, alcohol, drugs, and mindless engagement with technology, and, not surprisingly, it is filled with food. When used in this way, food deceives us into temporary comfort, even elation. Food triggers the hedonistic or pleasure center of our brain. In fact, food triggers the same receptors in the frontal lobe of the brain that are triggered by narcotics, alcohol, and nicotine. The result is a feeling of euphoria, pleasure, and comfort. *Momentarily.* But as it is transient, food leaves us wanting, urging us to engage again and again against our best judgement, against our bodies' knowing, to eat above and beyond what is necessary, resulting in self-harm and disease. Food is a simple comfort. It is easy, it is accessible, and it does not carry the negative stigma of drugs or excessive alcohol use. Food provides relief, albeit temporary, from difficult feelings, emotions, and emptiness. And, therefore, food is a common go-to to self-soothe.

We are primed from birth to have positive associations with food, and the co-mingling of food and love is literally hardwired in our physiology as oxytocin, the hormone responsible for the release of milk from the mother's breast, also fosters feelings of love and connection between mother and child. The dual role of oxytocin to provide nourishment and secure attachment solidifies the connection between food and love, food and comfort. Our social constructs also solidify this interconnection. Consider Grandma's warm chicken soup, a neighbor's fresh chocolate chip cookie, or Mom's special mac'n'cheese casserole. In these ways, food signifies love and family. Our rituals and traditions also revolve around food, and the communal meals at these occasions are an important way in which we experience our togetherness. Some of my fondest memories growing up are of experiencing togetherness around the table whether we were gathering for our nightly dinner or to a special meal, like Shabbat, Sunday brunches, or Thanksgiving. In all these occasions, food, family, and community were deeply interconnected. The sanctity of sharing a meal is deeply ingrained in so many of our traditions; it is no wonder that food comforts and soothes us.

But of course, food has a very practical function. Food is essential to life. It is substantive. And when abused, it is destructive. The right foods will support our bodies and our health while the wrong foods or *too much food* will make us feel sick, foggy, and bloated and will cause disease over the long run. Thus, food has a unique positioning. Food is sustenance *and* comfort. Food has the potential to improve our health *and* the potential for harm. As such, food forces us to reckon with duality and encourages us to achieve balance in how we eat and perhaps, too, in how we live. Considering this, food can be viewed as a paradigm for how we nourish ourselves more broadly.

In the many years of doing this work, I have come to understand that the desire to lose weight is a plea for something deeper, a yearning for a different way of living, a different way of being. *Hunger,* then, is the perfect word to describe this yearning, and *food* the perfect microcosm of our struggle. Our relationship with food is symbolic of deeper contemplations and of our relationship with ourselves. How do we care for ourselves? Are we worthy of the time and attention required for that care? What boundaries are necessary to support those healthy relationships? What true longing is our desire for food signaling? What do we seek to control, and what might we need to relinquish in order to achieve peace? Where have we abdicated our power, and how can we reclaim it? Is there a path for healing rather than numbing? And if not for food, then what are we really hungry for? Our reckoning with food can be a way of opening to these significant questions. And change in our relationship with food can be a spark for broader change, creating a rippling effect to other areas of our lives. This, for me, is the greatest beauty in this work.

I am humbled, when at times, patients look at me skeptically, as if to ask, "You too?"

As if to suggest that my being in this work somehow precludes me from this work. Of course, I am not immune. My relationship with food over the years has embodied many of these contemplations, spanning from overindulgence to over-restriction. As a child of an immigrant family, I used food to soothe my longing to belong. As an adult, I restricted food as a way to feign control over an all too disciplined lifestyle. And in the decades between, I experienced food in countless other ways that reflected my experience at the time.

As a physician I have had the unique privilege of being the recipient of many stories and have come to the realization that as different as we are, we are so very much the same. Our needs, wants, and desires, our longing, heartbreak, grief, struggles, and our worries are the same. And I have benefited greatly from recognizing our common humanity. It is, of course, from a place of shared humanity that we have the courage to dig and explore our own psyche. My hope is just that, by reading these stories, you too will recognize that your experiences are shared; you too will know that you are not alone. There is great power in that validation and in the vulnerability that it allows.

I imagine that if any of my patients happen to read this, they may think I am writing about them. Indeed, I am drawing from my experiences, both personal and professional, but the identities of my patients have been changed in these stories. I have turned the story of the teenage girl into the story of the grandma and the story of the retired professional into the story of the working mom. In some cases, the stories of two people were so similar that, in my own mind, they blended, and I myself could not distinguish one from another. That is to highlight, once again, the commonality of our experience and to say, patient or not, that I hope you see yourself in these stories and that you take refuge in the common thread that connects us all.

HUNGRY
FOR PERFECTION

I FELT AN ACHE in my chest as I watched her cry. It is not unusual for patients to cry in my office, given that our weight and our bodies are so tightly tied to our vulnerabilities. But that felt different. I felt a visceral reaction to witnessing Sofi's pain.

Sofi was in her early 20s, and her face was like that of a porcelain doll, striking yet childlike and innocent. She was wringing her hands as I walked into the exam room. I greeted her and offered her the opportunity to share the reason for her visit. It took her a moment to look up at me. The pause felt long and uncomfortable, but I remained quiet, aware of a stirring inside me. Finally, she began to speak, and, in that moment, I understood. In Sofi I could not help but see a younger version of myself.

Sofi was the oldest of three siblings. Her parents immigrated from Russia to the United States just before she was born. She understood their dreams and aspirations. And, also, their burdens and struggles. That part she understood deeply. Sofi sought to honor their struggle by being self-sufficient and self-reliant. She honored their struggle by being easily placated and satisfied. Sofi honored their struggle by not asking or wanting, by being responsible, being sensible, and by being diligent with her studies and with her help in the household. Sofi honored their struggle by striving for perfection in everything she did. This disposition had made her a *good girl*, but it also had made her weary. She had demanded too much of herself and rewarded too little. This she had gleaned from her education at home. Sofi's drive for perfection meant never doing enough, never achieving enough, never being enough. And finally, *that* burden had become too hard to carry.

As she shared her story, I suppressed the reflex to reassure her. How could I tell her that she would be enough the moment she allowed herself to be? That she did not need to please in order to be valued? That she was perfect as she was? That she *too* deserved to want and to need? How could I tell her that acknowledging her own needs was not weak or cowardly, but an act of bravery in and of itself? In order to keep giving, she needed to have something left to give.

Those are the things I wished to share, but I couldn't. Because they were not what Sofi wished to speak of. That is not what Sofi told me—that she is tired and weary, that she is relentless and unforgiving, that she longs to be valued, worthy and enough. What she told me is that she is fat.

Fat. Oh, how I detest that word.

I wished to admonish her, but I offered a smiling reproach instead.

The irony is that she was not *fat*, or obese or overweight, nor did she have excess weight by any clinical measure. There is a construct called *BMI*, or *body mass index*, that is imperfect but provides some measure to gauge a healthy range of weight for any given height. When I explained this to Sofi, that healthy weight is not a perfect number but a range, all she could do was grab the flesh at her belly to make her point.

Sofi has excelled at everything. What else could she possibly condemn other than some excess flesh? She did not know what I know now. That with this mindset nothing will ever be enough. I was just as critical of myself at size 2 as I was at size 10. I was nearing 40 when it first occurred to me that *enough* was a decision. I say *first occurred* because it would have to occur to me again and again, and *again*. Beliefs are stubborn that way. They come seemingly out of nowhere yet somehow get embedded in our psyche. The first step to challenging our beliefs is with curiosity to their origins because often they are not even our own. They originate from something we witnessed, something we were told, something we observed, or a position we felt compelled to take on. Over time these insidious beliefs become entrenched in our minds. This is an essential feature of their power, the subtlety with which they take root. Where had my belief of *not enough* come from? No one ever told me that I was not enough. My parents never scorned me about grades or expectations or how to make them proud. But then again, they did not have to. I did that on my own.

Perfectionism is a trait in which one's self-worth is dependent on achieving an unrealistic standard or goal. By definition, the standard is unattainable, leading the perfectionist to suffer from constant self-criticism and a belief of inherent unworthiness. In striving for the goal of *perfect*, perfectionists are unable to appreciate anything short of their ideal, as anything less is viewed as a failure. Perfectionism can have other features, such as fear of making mistakes, a perception of high parental expectations and criticism, excessive doubt over one's actions, and a strong desire for structure and order. Perfectionists often masquerade as high achievers, which in and of itself is not a problem. The difference is that the perfectionist will set unachievable goals that *cannot* be achieved and then are self-critical when they are not achieved. Falling short of their own unrealistic standards is then perceived as failure and undermines their self-worth. When they do achieve success, they cannot *see* their success. Perfectionists will invalidate their accomplishments as well as any praise they may receive. This may show itself as an inability to take credit or to hear compliments or praise. In this way they are unable to validate themselves, nor are they able to accept validation from others. In spite of the desire to achieve great success, perfectionists ironically often sabotage their own success. The fear of failure is so strong that perfectionists opt to play small, *get in their own way* rather than take a chance and risk failure. Or more commonly, they will simply just burn out. Perfection can be chased only so far before it is met with anxiety, depression, addiction, and disordered eating.

Where had Sofi's beliefs originated? Perhaps from something she heard or something that had been said? Perhaps they arose merely from her witnessing the sacrifices of her parents? Knowing the real truth behind the storyline is irrelevant because our stories are usually not based in truth. Nonetheless, we take their validity for granted, assuming wrongly that if we think it, then it must be true. The more we think these thoughts, the more entrenched and automatic they become until toxic patterns of thinking become habitual. These thoughts then motivate our behavior. Our beliefs manipulate our thoughts, which then influence our behavior.

I explained to Sofi that when it comes to weight-related beliefs, people who engage in negative thoughts about themselves create a self-fulfilling prophecy. Ironically, people who have negative beliefs about their weight and their bodies are less likely to engage in healthy practices that can change their weight. Studies have shown that people who have negative weight-related beliefs about themselves are less likely to choose healthy food or to participate in exercise or physical activity. Thus, negative thinking will undermine her desire for change.

While Sofi was not overweight, she did have an unhealthy pattern of eating that was inconsistent with her goals—weight or otherwise—that I believe stemmed in large part from her negative thought patterns. She alternated between overindulgence and over-restriction, which left her feeling physically uncomfortable and unhappy. Over the course of many visits, I encouraged Sofi to reframe her narrative. I asked her to consider if her negative thoughts about herself were really true. Could there perhaps be an alternative? I encouraged Sofi to create some space between herself and her thoughts, to separate herself so that she could play the role of an observer. From this perspective, she could take note of her thought patterns in a more detached and curious manner, allowing herself to cast doubt on them and create an alternate narrative.

I also wondered if she could acknowledge her true hunger. While her desire was for perfection, her *hunger* was for self-compassion. Sofi cared about her weight in that moment, but I had my eye more broadly on her wellbeing. I understood the perils of striving for perfection. Fortunately, a focus on self-compassion could address both her weight and her perfectionism. Studies have shown that mindful self-compassion can support healthy eating behaviors, behavior change, and weight regulation as well as increase intentions for healthier behaviors overall. But more importantly, studies have shown that self-compassion can diminish the negative effects of perfectionism on wellbeing. People with perfectionist tendencies who engage in self-compassion practices report greater subjective wellbeing overall. I wonder if she can adopt a mindset that does not judge or blame imperfection, but rather is cognizant that our imperfections, universal as they are, make us human.

Our imperfections don't make us flawed; they make us human.

It is only with self-compassion that she would be able to make the change that she sought, in a durable and self-sustaining way. It is only with self-compassion that she could attend to her true hunger. And only with self-compassion would she truly thrive.

Sofi, you are enough! I wished to say.

But *enough* is *her* decision. A decision that emanates from her willingness to challenge her thoughts and beliefs. Only when she chooses to detangle herself from this toxic pattern of thinking can she wrestle back her power. A decision that will follow when she addresses her hunger for self-compassion. I wished so strongly to redirect her, but Sofi was not ready. She recognized the impact of her negative thinking but was also afraid to let it go. She believes negative pressure and negative self-talk is motivating, gives her an edge, and feels that she is benefiting from this positioning. I can understand that too. People often confuse self-provocation with motivation.

In the end, I had to acknowledge my own desire to fix. I could not coerce or force her. This was Sofi's journey, and no matter how stirred I was by it, she would have to be ready. All I could do was create space for where she was at that moment and plant a seed that she would nourish.

I hoped that she did but would not know for certain because after our initial visit, I did not see Sofie again.

HUNGRY
FOR SELF-LOVE

"MY MOTHER BOUND HER breasts after I was born so that her milk would not come in," Lily said somewhat offhandedly.

"*Why?*" I ask.

Lily shrugged. "She said breastfeeding was gross. Besides, she would not have been able to diet if she were breastfeeding. She always did care about her body more than anything else," Lily said, seemingly immune to the irony of it all. Breastfeeding *is* associated with post-partum weight loss, after all, but I didn't mention that in the moment.

Just minutes before, Lily's mother had been sitting with us in the office before I asked to speak to Lily alone. I had to admonish myself not to be judgmental. It is one thing to have an adolescent with a hundred pounds of excess weight and type 2 diabetes whose weight loss is medically necessary—those cases are so challenging and heartbreaking—but it is quite another thing when the excess weight is minimal as was in Lily's case and the mother appears to be the driver of the desire to lose weight. Her mother was well-dressed, almost too much for the occasion. She looked as if she were plucked out of a magazine, all in black and designer labels, her hair blown out and curled, and her face made up impeccably.

It was a painful contrast to Lily, who sat beside her. Lily looked like she had rolled out of bed and left the house in her pajamas. Flannel drawstring pants, a tank top, and no bra. Her presentation screamed protest. It was clear that Lily had no interest in being at my office. I could almost imagine how she was dragged out of her house unwillingly. I'd smiled at Lily by way of invitation, but she said nothing. Wasting no time, her mother cut in.

"I just want her to be healthy, you know. I *love* her, and you can see she is so beautiful, *but...*"

But, I thought to myself.

"But...she has just gained so much weight, *too* much weight!"

As her mother continued to speak about her, my eyes remained on Lily. She sat frozen, slouched in the chair beside her mom, gazing steadfastly at her feet. Her shame was so present, it was palpable.

Can her mom feel it too? I wondered.

I secretly hated her mother but could concede that mothers are in a difficult position, guilty if we do too much, guilty if we do too little. My own mother never seemed to notice my struggle with my weight. I blamed her for not acknowledging my excess weight, for *not* having done anything. And I often wonder about my own children. How do *they* perceive my insistence on maintaining healthy habits and a healthy weight?

With her mother gone, I tried to engage Lily and address the heaviness in the room.

"It must be hard to hear your mom talk about you that way," I said.

She finally returned my gaze.

"She has been obsessed about my weight since I was 6." The grief on Lily's face was clear.

I recalled my own memory of when I was 6, travelling to New York to spend time with my family for the holidays. Food was always abundant in my grandmother's home, and I loved her cooking. I remember being called to the lavish spread on her table. As I excitedly filled my plate, someone grabbed the serving spoon from my hand. I looked above me to see an older woman, a family member I hardly knew, replace the spoon to the tray of food without even acknowledging me.

She turned to my mom. "You shouldn't let her eat so much," she said. "She is a big girl already."

I looked to my mother, but she said nothing. Cultural etiquette would favor respect of an elder over defense of a child. I recall the shame that flushed my face and filled my body as I stood there.

What do I do with the plate?

Certainly, I would not be able to eat with the humiliation rising like bile in the back of my throat.

Is everyone watching me?

I kept my face down, horrified that my eyes might meet theirs.

How can I back away from the table? How can I make myself so small that I cannot be seen? I felt so ashamed in that moment that I wanted to disappear.

Prior to that moment, it never occurred to me that my body was *big* or appeared that way to others. That's the thing about excess weight: there are few vulnerabilities that we wear on our sleeve, and this distinction is fundamental to the judgement and shame it evokes. People don't *look* diabetic, for example. I'm not even sure that I was overweight at 6, but that accusation planted a seed in my consciousness, one that would take root and flourish. I became fixated on my weight. And with every year, that preoccupation grew. By the time I was in middle school, I was completely absorbed in this negative self-impression, which was compounded by the usual adolescent uncertainties and insecurities.

If I were thin, would I belong? Would I have more friends? Would I be liked?

In my mind, everything rested on my belief that if I were thin, then...

And because I wasn't, I measured my words. I covered myself with concealing clothes. I thought twice about swimming parties, and when I did go, I didn't swim. I had misgivings about dance class and cheerleading squad because of the leotards and short skirts that were required. Everything I did was colored by my dissatisfaction with my body.

I imagined a 6-year-old Lily. I imagined her shame the day this belief became embedded in *her* mind. Her mother likely had her own damaging narrative around her body, which she handed down to her daughter. And perhaps, despite her mother, this belief would have taken hold in Lily anyway.

Body dissatisfaction affects nearly 50% of 13-year-olds and close to 80% of 17-year-old girls. Negative body perception can begin as early as 6 years of age and affects overweight, obese, and even *normal*-weight girls. One might think that underweight girls would be spared, but even they are not immune, as studies show that underweight girls also suffer from negative body image. Mother or not, negative body image is so pervasive that Lily would likely have suffered from it anyway. But I wondered, does it not carry a greater sting that it *was* her mother who had helped shape this narrative, one so cloaked in shame?

Fat shaming is rampant in every domain of our society and impairs not only the emotional wellbeing, but also the physical wellbeing of the person being degraded. Studies show that fat shaming is perceived by the body as a type of stress, leading to elevations of cortisol as well as metabolic dysfunction. Unfortunately, shame is used as a form of motivation, by parents, by physicians, by health care providers, and by society at large. But as shame researcher Brene' Brown famously articulates, "You cannot shame people into change." In fact, shame will have the opposite effect.

Studies show that weight bias and discrimination increase the likelihood for weight gain and obesity, even if the individual is considered normal weight to begin with. Fat shaming is associated with anxiety, depression, disordered eating, and poor lifestyle habits overall. The consequences become even more harmful when negative bias is internalized. Those with high levels of weight-bias internalization will suffer 3 times the likelihood of developing metabolic syndrome independent of weight and other related risk factors. Studies also show that those who are subject to this type of discrimination will be more likely to die from any cause.

I was not concerned about Lily's weight. I was more concerned about what *she* thought about her weight and how that had affected her relationship with food, her relationship with her body, and her relationship with herself. If this was not addressed, it could potentially result in disordered eating, depression, and other mental health concerns, if it had not already. As it turns out, even though her mother was the impetus for the visit, Lily was very preoccupied with her body. She admitted, at times she spent hours looking at herself in the mirror and scrutinizing how she looks. She changed outfits repeatedly in order to find the "right fit" and felt like this is such an undertaking that it kept her from getting to places on time and sometimes immobilized her altogether. Her mood was highly dependent on how she believed she looked or, as she said, "on how fat I am that day." She described super highs when she felt "thin," followed by steep lows when she felt "fat." As if all aspects of her life were viewed through the lens of her body shape and size.

My suspicions had been correct: Lily was suffering mental health consequences related to her body image and met criteria for body dysmorphic disorder. Body dysmorphic disorder (BDD) is characterized by hyper-focus on one's physical appearance as well as repetitive or compulsive behaviors such as mirror checking, excessive grooming, and even skin picking, which I later learned that Lily engaged in as well. I insisted that the best course of action was for her to see a therapist and maybe a psychiatrist for medications. But she was not amenable, nor would she allow me to discuss it with her mother. Lily's parents and apparently Lily herself had negative perceptions of therapy. What was even more difficult was that I had already been forewarned by her mom that if Lily wasn't *going to take this seriously* and lose weight, then they would not be paying for it. While no longer a minor, Lily was beholden to her parents financially. How could I reconcile her mother's insistence on weight loss with Lily's overall health and wellbeing? How could I reconcile Lily's insistence on weight loss without contributing to her preoccupation with her body? I wondered if Lily could tease out her self-perception from her mother's perception of her and her body. And I wondered if Lily could motivate herself from a place of self-love rather than a place of shame?

I ended the visit with Lily's mom again. I explained to her that as a mother of a teenager myself, I knew parental involvement would hinder our process but promised that I would involve her if needed. Fortunately, her mother was pacified, and she agreed to not interfere. I was also able to negotiate a few ground rules with Lily. She insisted on being weighed. We agreed that I would weigh her but would not share her weight with her, at least at first, and that she could not weigh herself at home. If she could trust me to be the keeper of the numbers, I promised to redirect our plan if her goals were not being met. I also broached the topic of therapy again. I suspected her negative perceptions stemmed from her parents. She had access to the free mental health resources on her college campus and could make the decision to start therapy independent of her parents. She agreed to take it under consideration. I also reserved the option of starting an SSRI (selective serotonin reuptake inhibitor), which would help her mood as well as body dysmorphia, if needed.

In order to reach Lily, I had to align, as always is the case, with something she cared about deeply. That value was her education. In our conversations, Lily had relayed her desire to become a marine biologist. We shared a love of science and biology. She also told me that lack of focus had always been a problem for her, and she had always wondered if she had some form of ADD or ADHD. This was another fortunate circumstance because I was able to bring her academic interests into the plan. I shared with her that while I studied incessantly, I did not study effectively. I told Lily that I wished I knew then some of the ways in which I could have been a more efficient student. She was intrigued.

It turns out that the same things that are good for our bodies are also good for our minds. Research shows that simple measures such as increasing fruits and veggies in our diet improves focus and productivity. Omega-3 fatty acids found in fish improve mood and cognition. As do the B vitamins found in leafy greens. Could Lily notice how her diet affected mood? Did sugar make her lethargic? Did protein and the fiber in complex carbohydrates help her focus?

I also shared the abundant data showing the academic benefit of exercise. Studies consistently show that exercise improves concentration, memory, cognitive function, and test scores. I shared my own aha moment when I noticed running enhanced my focus while studying. The focus on her academic success resonated with Lily and took attention away from her body to her academic pursuits. With time Lily became more in tune with how her behaviors make her feel and work as opposed to focusing on her shape and her weight.

But what I really wanted Lily to understand was this:

You cannot shame your way into change.

This narrative of shame might have started with her mother, but it was up to Lily to put an end to it. She could either perpetuate the story line or come up with her own. I wanted her to know that she might not be able to change her mother, but she could change her relationship with herself with a practice of self-love. Cooking nourishing food for herself was an act of self-love. Making time for movement was an act of self-love. Uplifting her spirits with nature, a good book, or heartfelt conversation with a positive influence in her life was an act of self-love. And only through self-love could she ultimately put aside the mirror checking, the clothes changing, the skin picking, and the self-loathing.

Fortunately, in the end, Lily's mom did allow her to start seeing a therapist, an addition that I was grateful for. Slowly, Lily began to shift. Her lifestyle began to shift, her habits began to shift, and her disposition began to shift. While we never did discuss the numbers on the scale, by the end of the year, Lily had lost around 10 pounds. More importantly, Lily is thriving. She changed her major to psychology and moved away to Stanford for her master's degree. At our last communication, Lily told me about a curriculum she developed for high school girls, addressing negative body image and mental wellbeing. She hopes to teach others through her experience that acknowledging a hunger for self-love can break the cycle of shame and allow, instead, a healthy relationship to develop between food, their body, and themselves.

Hungry
for Soothing

Ricky was a 36-year-old with a huge personality. He is affable and charming and had me laughing before we sat down across from one another.

No sooner had he seated himself than he started with this: "Look doc," he said, leaning in and draping his arms over my desk. "I don't have an issue. I don't eat ice cream because I am depressed and I don't go to the drive thru for hamburgers and french fries. I'm Italian, and we just love good food. We love our pasta, you know what I'm sayin'?"

Yes, of course I knew. I love pasta too.

Ricky's taste for food was indulgent. He described eating at the best and most decadent restaurants. Steak, lobster, paella, fettuccine dripping in cream sauce. Those were just some of the foods he had enjoyed that week alone. He took pleasure in it and was not interested in stopping. It wasn't only his food that was decadent; so was his lifestyle. Ricky was quick to share that he had quit a prestigious position as a hedge fund manager to trade stocks from home.

"Who needs that kinda' life," he says, "when you can be making just as much by sleeping in and day-trading?"

He didn't have a girlfriend or wife, just *a bunch of babes* whom he romanced in succession. Even his hobbies were indulgent. Ricky told me that he had a collection of cars, *lots of cars,* so many that he had built an underground garage to store those he prized most. Ricky made it perfectly clear that he was happy how he was. His weight was not an issue and did not affect his life. Unlike those who suffer social isolation, bias, or prejudice due to their excess weight, Ricky did not, and, indeed, he did seem content in every aspect of his life. Even his health was unaffected. Despite being over 100 pounds overweight, Ricky had a perfectly clean bill of health. True, statistically he was more likely to develop diabetes or another obesity-related condition, but this is not always the case, and Ricky could certainly remain healthy and unaffected by his weight for the rest of his life. Given this, maybe the incentive for change was just not present?

"I could stop eating if I wanted to," he said as if to answer my thoughts, "but I don't want to. Who wants to eat like a rabbit?"

"So why are you here, Ricky?" I asked.

"I really don't know." He shrugged nonchalantly.

Ricky told me that his mother had given him my information and asked him to call. But as he sat before me, he realized that he did not really see any reason to be there.

But something told me otherwise.

He had made it to the office, had he not? If he really did not want to be there, why would he have taken time out of his day to come? I was not yet ready to let him go.

Earlier in our conversation, he had shared that he was born in San Diego, as was I. I decided to revisit this point of sameness as a way to re-engage him and buy some time. After some discussion about the beauty of the city in which we were both born, I was able to circle back to his childhood. He had mentioned that his father was in the army and stationed at Camp Pendleton around the time he was born. Following my intuition, I referenced his being raised by a sergeant, sharing that while my father had not been in the army, he was raised like a soldier and, in turn, so was I.

I noted a change in his demeanor with my candid disclosure. Ricky shifted in his chair. And then retorted with a chuckle: "Nothing like having an army man for a father, right?"

If his feigned laugh had fooled me, his down-trodden look did not. I could tell I had hit on something. Something that told me that his pleasure seeking was in fact not seeking pleasure for the sake of pleasure but for the sake of anesthetizing. He was seeking pleasure in order to *soothe*.

I understood what it felt like to live in an over-disciplined home. My father's experience of having been raised in a boarding school most of his childhood had colored his parenting. He was stern and austere and had a capricious temper. Despite his ultra-disciplinarian nature, he was an engaged and dedicated parent. I have pictures of him holding me up by the nape of my jacket as I was learning to take my first steps much like he held on to the handles of my bike, running to keep up, when we took off my training wheels for the first time. My dad was the one who took me to the doctor for my chronic stomach aches and the one who casually reviewed the sex-ed pamphlet I brought home in the 5th grade. As an adult, I turned to him when I agonized over school, and his was the shoulder I cried on when the pain of mommy-guilt was too much to bear. I shared with him my trials and tribulations, and he listened like a girlfriend would, intently and patiently.

But despite his softness in those moments, I feared him. It was a reverential kind of fear, born of respect and a desire to please. I would do what was expected, and the expectations were many. I was raised with strict rules and abided by stricter standards. I was to be studious, polite, presentable, and obedient. Always obedient—I would not protest regardless of how nonsensical his mandates—talking back was not an option. Trick or treating, excessive *chit-chat* on the phone, boys—these were just some of the many things that were not allowed. Summer was for summer school and the dreaded supplemental homework he provided. It never dawned on him that perhaps solving math problems involving trains at competing speeds or chemical mixtures at various dilutions was just not age appropriate. Indeed, he was both loving and terribly unyielding at once.

My father was passionate. His absence from his family at such a young age when he was in boarding school stoked, I imagine, his unyielding loyalty to them. He had a love for family that was deep and intense. You could see it in his eyes when they would visit or even at the mere mention of them. I welcomed the moments when I would sit on his lap and he would wrap his arms around me or when I would lay between him and my mother in bed to watch Sunday morning cartoons. And my favorite, when he would brush my face with his lashes and then bring his face to mine so that I could do the same. I basked in the warmth of those moments.

He was just as passionate in his anger as he was in his love. Temperamental and quick to provocation. His anger was hard to anticipate and even harder to prevent, but that made me only more willing to try. As a result, I developed a sort of radar, a hypervigilance for the feelings of others. Cultivating this 6th sense allowed me to anticipate aggravation, prophylax discontent, and smooth over any potential disruption. It was a skill that I carried into my work, my relationships, and really into all aspects of my life. But my desire to soothe those around me came at the cost of my own self-soothing. In service to others, I dismissed my own need for reassurance and comfort. Invariably, this resulted in a desire to soothe with food.

In listening to Ricky, it dawned on me that his indulgent lifestyle—the decadent food, penchant for fast cars, fast money, and *babes*—was a way to quiet the rumblings of his inner world. His desire for pleasure was born not only from his bodily desires but also in the service of quelling his emotions. What made Ricky seek so much pleasure was a hunger to soothe.

Ricky argued that he loved food and found pleasure in indulgence, period. Most people find pleasure in indulgent food. But not consistently and at the expense of their wellbeing. Ricky admitted to having gained 10 pounds in just that past year. Even if his weight had not affected his health overtly, how could it not affect his sleep, his mobility, or his comfort in some way? There is pleasure in food, but there is also pleasure in securing our health and our vitality. This knowing is the antidote to engaging excessively in pleasure to our own detriment.

My acknowledgment of the possibility of a stringent upbringing creates an opening, and Ricky readily shares his experience. Unlike my experience, his relationship with his father had always been strained, and he tells me they had been estranged for many years. Ricky was seeking pleasure as a way to alleviate his pain. His pain over a father with whom he never saw eye to eye. His pain over a father who could never be satisfied or appeased and from whom he never felt unconditional love.

Perhaps Ricky could begin to acknowledge that hunger, his hunger to soothe that pain.

Ricky agreed to our working together on his weight, but the process, as is often the case, was tangential, two steps forward and one step back. Several months went by, and Ricky shared that his father had been diagnosed with pancreatic cancer, a quick and terminal disease. He decided to leave for New York to spend time with him. I was sorry for unfortunate circumstances and for the interruption but knew that amends with his father would address his true hunger, his hunger to soothe.

HUNGRY
FOR ROUTINE

HARPER HAD RETURNED HOME from college nearly a year ago and was in a rut. She was not depressed, just apathetic and bored. Her major in public relations had not yielded any exciting job prospects, and she was unsure about the graduate degree that she was considering. Her indifference was exacerbated by the fact that she had moved back into her parents' home, and while they were supporting her financially, they were also *annoying* her with their constant questioning and interference in her affairs. Harper had picked up a job baby-sitting for an old family friend as a way to appease them, but other than that she didn't have much going on.

She told me that while she gained only 5-ish pounds as opposed to the "freshman 15," in college, since she returned home, she'd been gaining weight at a rapid pace.

"Twenty pounds!" she said, incensed. "I have gained 20 pounds since I've been home!"

I inquired about her daily activities.

"I don't really like to wake up early," Harper said, "so I sleep in until noon when I have to get myself ready for work."

"What time do you go to sleep?" I asked, curious if insomnia was driving this late start to the day.

"It depends. Sometimes 1 or 2, sometimes I'm up till 4 am."

"Because you can't sleep," I asked, concerned.

"No, sometimes I'm bingeing on Netflix or on my phone."

"So, when do you eat?"

It turns out that Harper did not have a routine for eating. Sometimes, she grabbed something on the way to work, sometimes she skipped breakfast. In fact, Harper did not have a schedule around anything that she did; her diet, her activity, her sleep, and even her work followed no set schedule.

The burning question in my mind was, where was Harper's routine, and how was this affecting her physical and mental wellbeing? How was it contributing to her weight gain and to her apathy? I knew that it is a significant contributor.

Routine, while seemingly mundane, is an important factor in cultivating happiness as well as health and productivity. All things that Harper was in desperate need of.

Routine has always been a big part of my life. Not intentionally, but more as a function of my reality. Between my rigorous work schedule and studies and my early start as a wife and mother, I had no choice but to commit to a structured routine. But I was also indoctrinated into adherence to routines in my upbringing. My father's boarding school sensibilities did not allow for haphazard meanderings in his children, and this ended up being a good thing, but admittedly, I did yearn for unstructured time. I finally got the opportunity the summer between my second and third year of medical school, right after I was married. I was so excited. I would have to study for my board exams but taking a month off school gave me lots of free time. I planned to sleep in, cook dinners, and exercise, of course, and I hoped to get into a long-desired creative project, jewelry making. I went to a local bead shop and purchased tiny colorful beads and beautiful exotic stones, special twine, and instruments. Perhaps it was too ambitious, but I craved leisure. At first, I convinced myself that

I should rest. I did get caught up on some much-needed sleep, but other than that spent most of my day wandering around my apartment. Every time I thought of exercise, I negotiated that I could do it later. When I thought to shop for dinner, I convinced myself we could order in even though that was not our style. Even during our most busy days, we committed to making our own meals. And as for the beads, well, nearly 25 years later, they are still in their packages somewhere in my garage. It turned out that without routine I had trouble doing anything at all. One might argue that I just needed downtime—that's in fact what I told myself. But I found as I passed the days aimlessly that I did not feel more rested. I felt more restless, my mood suffered, and my energy levels fell. By the end of the month, I was completely listless and dysphoric. It turns out that even leisure time requires structure and routine.

One thing the most successful people in history have in common is routine. Mr. Rogers is said to have woken up every morning at 5 am for prayer and contemplation. Beethoven counted out 60 beans every day for his morning coffee, and Steve Jobs started each day by making his bed. But routine is important for not only success but also happiness and wellbeing. When we create routine, we are more likely to adhere to the activities that bring us long-term joy and gratification. We know that wholesome food is in our best interest and it *feels* good when we eat well, and yet if we don't have a routine of meal planning and prepping by maintaining healthy ingredients in the fridge or packing a healthy lunch, we are less likely to eat the good food that we intend to. We know that daily movement and exercise improves our mood and is important to our wellbeing, but, again, if we don't plan for it and incorporate it as a daily routine, we are more likely to negotiate ourselves out of it. The same can be said for family dinners, quality time with friends, and even time for leisure. Without planning structured time for any of these activities, we are unlikely to engage in them in a consistent way. Creating routine reaffirms our intentions and combats the non-committal mindset that makes us indecisive. Without routine we are much more likely to negotiate with ourselves, which is exhausting in and of itself. It is much easier to just act than to think about, anticipate, and bargain over the action we intend to do. Negotiation causes fatigue, apprehension, and listlessness all while steering us away from what we intuitively know and need.

Routine helps us foster a feeling of familiarity and safety, which has a calming effect. In fact, adhering to routines has been shown to activate the parasympathetic nervous system, promoting rest and relaxation. Without routine we are more prone to reactivity, and impulsive decisions are rarely aligned with what truly gratifies us. And finally, routine is essential to creating long-term habits. Habits do not become habitual until they first become a routine. We must commit, consistently and continuously, to that which serves us until it becomes second nature.

I had to address Harper's lack of routine as a pre-requisite for the weight loss she desired. More importantly, I needed to address Harper's lack of routine in order to get her out of the *rut* in which she was robbing herself of her time and energy. Together, we made a list of the things she wished to change—financial independence so she could move out of her parents' house, feeling more energy, feeling more upbeat, and, of course, losing weight. It turns out that her wish list could in part (if not all) be addressed through consistent routine. I asked her to rank her list in order of importance and value and then helped her with an action plan to address her goals. We agreed that in order to make this a reality, she needed to change her behaviors. In order to feel energized, she needed to eat food that sustained her as opposed to skipping meals or eating foods that would leave her irritable and lethargic. We also agreed that she needed to limit screen time and sleep earlier so she could wake up earlier and take advantage of her time to job search or exercise. That would not only be good for her body but also would help her clear her head, improve her mood and outlook, and make her better able to take advantage of potential opportunities. While these goals may not all seem aligned with weight loss (you will read in the upcoming chapters that they are), but they addressed her hunger. A hunger for routine that in the end would keep her from losing weight and would contribute to further weight gain.

Within 6 months, Harper had not only lost her excess weight but also, more importantly, had secured a job, found a roommate, and was able to move out and live on her own. Incorporating routine allowed her to achieve not only her health goals but also her life goals. In my experience, these are often one and the same.

HUNGRY
FOR ABUNDANCE

DEBORAH RETURNED TO MY office after a long break. We had been working together since her sophomore year in college when she was referred for weight loss before a hernia repair. Deborah had had multiple surgeries for severe Crohn's disease, which had resulted in a large incisional hernia. But given her nutritional deficiencies and excess weight, her surgeon had advised that she work with me first to reduce her risk of complications. Fortunately, the surgery was elective, so we had time to work together.

Deborah steadily improved her diet, and we addressed her vitamin and nutrient deficiencies. Within a year, she lost approximately 20 pounds. Soon after we met, she moved to New York for graduate school, so we continued to work together in a hybrid of virtual and in-person visits where Deborah would see me in person when she was visiting. On one particular spring break, Deborah cancelled her appointment and did not reach out until months later.

"I blew it over Passover," she said as soon our video conference connected. "I always blow it over Passover."

It was true that since I had known Deborah, the religious holidays were always challenging. I could understand why, given that the holidays convened around food—family traditions so often do. But that day, Deborah shared another layer that we had never addressed.

"My family celebrated Passover in hiding," Deborah told me.

Deborah's mother was a young child in Poland when World War II erupted. Her grandmother recounted painful memories of hunger and near starvation. Instead of the homemade meals Deborah's grandmother was known for, the family survived on scraps that her grandfather gathered from a nearby barn.

"My grandmother always prepares so much food for the holidays," Deborah said. "And when I was younger, she would get upset if I did not eat it. My mom would get angry if left food on my plate. She would call me wasteful and disrespectful. 'Eat now because you may not have food tomorrow,' she would say. I remember being worried, even scared that would be true."

While I do not share the legacy of the Holocaust, I know how deeply food is ingrained in our traditions, our customs, and our family dynamics. I also know that consuming a meal can be just as much a show of love and respect as making the meal, while not eating what has been prepared for you, a sign of withholding. I too remember being encouraged to eat more than I needed, being encouraged not to waste, and being reminded that others were less fortunate than I, as a guilt-laden motivation to finish all the food on my plate.

In listening to Deborah's family history, I was reminded about a time early in my marriage. My grandmother, as was her practice, would show her love and respect for my new husband through food that she made. She would cook in abundance, reserving the first offering for him. On one occasion, she made *dolmeh*, a particularly labor-intensive dish consisting of a rice mixture of savory ingredients including mint, parsley, turmeric, saffron, tart cherry, raisins, and other dried fruits steamed together then stuffed into edible skins like grape leaves, emptied quince shells, cooked cabbage leaves or onion skins. He politely declined, offering that it did not sit well with him. While the explanation was logical and sensitive, she was visibly taken aback. Later, she would pull me aside and ask if she had done anything to upset him. As if his refusal was a show of personal disregard. It is a story we laugh about now, but in retrospect, it is exemplary of how deeply food is tied into our concept of family, love, and belonging.

Many years later, I asked my grandmother and the women of the family to come over for a *dolmeh*-making party. I thought this was an opportunity to learn how to make this dish and to create an experience out of cooking together. As I watched my grandmother effortlessly package handfuls of mixed rice into their delicate packages, I noted that my every memory of my grandmother involved food. At our celebrations, during our heartbreak, at every *Shabbat*, and during high holidays she is always cooking. Even when my grandfather was dying and was discharged from the hospital to spend his last days at home, she asked that his bed be set up by the kitchen, where she remained at his side, all the while cooking quietly at the stove. This had always been her way ever since she was a young child.

My grandmother was orphaned at the age of 6 when an unknown illness took her mother's life. She was the youngest of five sisters, who, motherless, were mostly in pursuit of their own interests. Her father soon remarried to a less than charitable woman, and it was in that setting that my grandmother received an education in homemaking, and in *cooking*. In the midst of this tragedy, my grandmother's sister nearest in age to her died suddenly, leaving behind a toddler and an infant. My grandmother was asked to help. She would visit them daily, tending to her nieces and her sister's husband. She smiles as she recounts that even then he had loved her cooking. It became clear that these children would need a mother, and the widower would need a wife. As was customary at the time, my grandmother took her sister's place to become at once a mother and bride at the young age of 11.

As she continues to wrap the *dolmeh* methodically, I see that her cooking has always been an expression of that service. When my grandmother cooks, she cooks lavishly. As if the abundance at her table is demonstrative of her martyrdom and our consuming it an acknowledgment. I imagined that for Deborah's grandmother, it was the same. Her cooking was in service to her family, an embodiment of her sacrifice, imbued with the pain of her past, and her family's partaking of the meal was an acknowledgement of that sacrifice.

We have evolved from hunters and gatherers who lived in a time of food scarcity, and as a result, we have evolved mechanisms to preserve energy. These mechanisms make it physiologically difficult to rid ourselves of excess calories and weight. When we lose weight, an adaptive response against starvation is triggered in our bodies. Hunger hormones rise, driving us to consume more. Our metabolic rate or "metabolism" drops to reduce energy expenditure. Our fat cells, the storage depots for energy excess, become even more skillful at extracting fat from our circulation and storing it in our bodies as more fat. Our bodies have evolved physiologically to adapt to scarcity, and so have our minds but not our mindset. We have maintained a *mindset* of scarcity, a fear of scarcity despite relative plenty. And it causes us to react with excess. Consider how most respond to free food in the workplace, handouts at the grocery, unlimited access at a buffet. Our response is much like the impulse to clear our plate of food. We feel compelled to overeat. However, most of us are not lacking nutrients. There will always be more dessert, more dinners, another opportunity to partake. Knowing this, we should be able to operate from a mind place of abundance rather than fear.

Food scarcity gets ingrained not only in our thoughts but also in our genes. Scientific studies show scarcity of nutrients while in utero can alter the expression of genes in a growing fetus, increasing the risk of metabolic diseases down the line. Epigenetics describes the way in which the expression of our genes is affected by environmental factors. Studies in animals and humans are increasingly making clear that the parents' diet can alter the expression of genes in this "epigenetic" way, altering the genes of the offspring, which can then be passed in turn to their offspring.

This phenomenon was clearly demonstrated in individuals conceived during the Dutch Hunger Winter in the 1940s. Medical records of individuals who were exposed to famine and severe caloric restriction while in utero reveal epigenetic changes in a specific gene involved in human growth and development called insulin-like growth factor II (IGFII). The severe caloric restriction experienced in the fetus resulted in fewer genetic copies of this hormone as compared to siblings who were conceived before or after the famine. Affected individuals had greater cardiovascular and metabolic disease later in life, including abnormal blood glucose and cholesterol and a doubling in their rate of cardiovascular disease. Multigenerational studies have shown that the negative effects of poor nutrition were not limited to the first generation of children exposed to famine but were transmitted to second and third generations as well. Studies have shown that even grand-progeny of women exposed to famine had a higher rate of obesity as compared to children who were not exposed to famine in utero, suggesting that maternal food insufficiency has far-ranging effects on health and disease in not only the affected generation but also the generations to follow. And so, scarcity gets passed down in story and substance.

The reverse is also true. Dietary excess in either parent can result in epigenetic changes that affect the offspring's likelihood of obesity as well. In fact, poor maternal diet can affect children's dietary preferences throughout their life. In one study, mothers who were given a diet consisting of donuts, cakes, pies, and potato chips during pregnancy or lactation had offspring who consistently showed a greater preference for high-fat foods as compared to those moms who were given a healthy diet during this critical time. This and similar data suggest that taste preferences are pre-programmed and are in part dependent on the food choices of the mother. In addition, studies have shown that parents who are obese are more likely to have obese children. While familial diet and other environmental factors play a role, it is increasingly believed that epigenetic phenomenon increase the likelihood and propensity of obesity in offspring. In fact, epigenetics is now considered to be an important contributor to the generational increase of obesity. Molecular studies show that nutritional excess in the perinatal period affect the number and growth of fat cells in the progeny so that children of obese parents are born with a higher number of fat cells. Nutritional excess in a parent has been shown also to alter the child's brain's response to hunger cues such that hunger, appetite, and body weight are increased in the offspring throughout his or her life. Thus, what we eat becomes hardwired in our children, reflecting how and what *they* eat and in their future health.

Many of us were taught that food was scarce. Perhaps like Deborah, we were told stories of our grandparents wanting for food. Maybe they grew up during the Holocaust or Great Depression or maybe they were immigrants who escaped civil war as mine did. Many have personal experiences of poverty and food scarcity themselves. And others still have a narrative around food that reflects sacrifice and martyrdom. Because of this, we are conditioned to clean our plate, to finish off our children's leftovers, or to partake in food because it is free or just there, in each example eating more than we needed or wanted to. This impulse is learned and originates from a history based in scarcity and fear. But when we act from a place of fear, we cannot act with intention.

There are many unfortunate among us who are lacking for food. But many of us who fear scarcity are not lacking. We have enough. I do not endorse waste, but when we feel compelled to eat out of any feeling other than hunger, we *are* being wasteful. We are being wasteful with our own health.

How does a mindset of abundance reframe our narrative around food? What if we changed our view from how much food we *can* consume to how much we *chose* to consume? How can we see this act of self-care as also an act of service to our children? In doing so, we can shift the narrative from fear to empowerment, from scarcity to abundance.

Yet Deborah's actions appeared to come from a deeper layer of scarcity from within which manifested an inability to recognize her needs and prioritize them over the needs or emotions of others. Deborah's keen attention to her grandmother's needs was at the exclusion of her own self-interest. Of course, Deborah wished to be sensitive to her grandmother, but by consistently prioritizing her grandmother, Deborah was reinforcing the notion that she doesn't matter. I encouraged Deborah that she could do both. She could consider her grandmother while considering herself as well. When we operate from a place of abundance, we create a spaciousness that is available and inclusive of all.

And so, when it comes to our children, we can be aware of the ways in which our view of, positioning of, and language around food, both implicit and explicit, impact our children's view. By not compelling our children to experience fear or guilt around food, we can prevent food from becoming an emotional pawn transmitting the burden of our own scarcity. Speaking about food in terms of an abundance and eating for health and wellbeing will establish a mindset around food that aligns with our deepest values to be well and live well.

Fortunately, despite their past experiences, both her mother and grandmother were supportive of Deborah's efforts to improve her health, and when she shared her concerns with them, they were receptive and responsive. Deborah's insight into her family's narrative was instrumental to navigating her hunger. Recognizing that her Passover meal was not only communal but also the embodiment of a food narrative of scarcity allowed her to disengage from that inheritance and to distinguish true hunger from guilt and fear of reprisal and from her grandmother's need to be validated. Deborah continued to work with me with a renewed energy and without further disruptions. By her next in-person visit the following summer, Deborah had achieved her goal weight and was able to undergo surgery as planned.

HUNGRY
FOR NATURE

EMILY DID NOT COME to see me for weight loss. If anything, she needed to gain weight. She had steadily been losing weight over the previous 4 months, and because she was already fairly thin, the additional weight loss had put her at risk of being underweight. Emily is otherwise young and healthy, but about 6 months earlier she started to develop a constellation of bothersome symptoms: upset stomach, constipation—but sometimes diarrhea—nausea, occasional vomiting, insomnia, hair loss, and intermittent hives, which were present on the day's exam as well. Emily had had a whole slew of tests and exams, including an endoscopy, which yielded no diagnosis. She was following a gluten-free, no-dairy diet that did not seem to have made much of an impact, but she was still worried that her diet or perhaps a food allergy or nutrient deficiency might be causing her symptoms. She brought with her a large manilla envelope filled with many, *many* pages of test results.

There was a lot to tease out, particularly the symptoms. We are taught Occam's razor in medical school, the principle that despite multiple symptoms in a patient, the greatest likelihood is that a single diagnosis is explanatory, rather than multiple diagnoses. But in my experience, these symptoms usually don't come about all at once, and sometimes, patients develop new symptoms along the way. Sometimes, new symptoms are a side effect of the treatments or medications prescribed or a side effect of feeling unwell for so long. Invariably, when symptoms become chronic, anxiety contributes in some degree to the overall symptomatology, and this can show up in many different ways, including how we eat, what we eat, and how much we eat.

That appeared to be the case with Emily, and as I spoke with her, that is what I gathered. Her first symptom was stomach pain, which was made worse when she ate or drank. As a result, she became fearful of eating and limited her food intake dramatically. Perhaps this is what caused the constipation? She was then seen by a gastroenterologist who gave her medications for reflux as well as pretty heavy doses of a prescription laxative. At those doses, laxatives can definitely cause stomach churning, nausea, and diarrhea. This only made Emily want to eat less. As the nausea got worse, she returned to the doctor and was given medication for it.

The medication he originally prescribed was not covered by her insurance, so she was given an older, cheaper alternative. I first learned about Compazine on an inpatient psychiatry rotation since it is also used as an anti-psychotic. It is a terrible drug with lots of side effects, not to mention it can worsen constipation. How often was she taking this "as needed" medication? It turns out Emily was so afraid of throwing up that she was taking it every day, sometimes multiple times per day. Her hair loss could certainly be explained by sudden weight loss or undoubtedly the stress of it all, which could also explain her insomnia and hives.

I wondered what was happening in Emily's life when the symptoms started and about her life in general. When I asked about her parents or who might be taking care of her then, she told me that she lived alone. Emily pulled out her phone to show me a photo of her family in a picturesque setting. She hadn't been back to Utah for nearly 2 years. That's when she was promoted within her company. Emily had never intended to work in the corporate offices of an international vacation rental company. Her first job was as an instructor at a local ski lodge in Utah, where her family still lives. She worked there during ski season, teaching kids how to ski and snowboard. Her love of skiing and the outdoors made that the perfect job for her while she was in high school, and even in college she would return during her breaks to teach. Her passion for skiing and her gentle way with the kids made her well known among visitors of the lodge and soon among her bosses and her bosses' bosses too. When she graduated, Emily was offered a job at the corporate headquarters in Los Angeles. Her dedication was not limited to the ski slopes, and she found herself quickly ascending the corporate ranks too. Her success led her to long hours under the fluorescent lights in a sterile office, and this, of course, was not to her liking. Emily longed for the mountains. She longed for the snow. She longed for the majestic trees. And she hungered for nature.

Looking at the pictures of her home, I could see why. Having lived in Southern California for over 30 years, I too longed for the beauty of changing seasons—rain and fallen leaves and snow. I had learned in recent years how important nature was to my wellbeing. After years of schooling and wife-*ing* and doctoring and mothering, I decided to take a weekend trip to a retreat lodge in the California redwoods. I had always known that I loved the trees, but my weekend among them reminded me how impactful time in nature could be. When I returned, I made a promise to incorporate nature more routinely into my life. I did not have to travel; nature was all around me. The ocean, hiking trails in the mountains, or even time spent on my front porch when the early-morning dew gives rise to the smell of acorns and eucalyptus, these all had a deeply calming impact on me as if to reset my nervous system.

The data supports this notion. Nature really does reset the nervous system. In one study, researchers looked at the effect of nature in acute stress recovery by studying subjects who had watched a stressful movie followed by either a video of a natural setting or a video of urban settings. Physiologic variables of stress including heart rate, muscle tension, skin conductance, and pulse transit time, which is a surrogate measure of blood pressure, were measured in both groups. Researchers found that merely *viewing* videos of nature resulted in significant reductions in these variables of stress. The authors concluded that exposure to nature prompted the parasympathetic or "rest and relax" part of our nervous system, buffering the sympathetic stress response to the initial stressful movie. Furthermore, they suggested that their results were consistent with the psycho-evolutionary theory—that nature influences a positively toned emotional state and results in positive changes in our physiology.

Spending time in nature also has psychological benefits. Greater interactions with nature are associated with reduced depressive symptoms, anxiety, and psychologic stress. Exposure to nature has also been shown to enhance our cognition and productivity just as being in the outdoors is associated with better attention, focus, memory, and cognitive function in general. In fact, in one study of children diagnosed with ADHD, a 20-minute walk in a park resulted in better concentration and focus as determined by cognitive testing as compared to those children who walked in an urban setting. In another study, college students were given a range of cognitive tests before and after a 50-minute walk either in a park or in an urban setting and found that those students who walked in a park showed a marked improvement in cognitive testing as compared to those who walked in urban settings.

Finally, spending time in nature has been shown to reduce cardiometabolic disease and mortality as well. In a large meta-analysis, increased greenspace exposure was associated with decreased blood pressure and reduced occurrence of type II diabetes, cardiovascular mortality, and all-cause mortality. The study found the incidence of stroke, hypertension, dyslipidemia, asthma, and coronary heart disease were all reduced in subjects who had greater exposure to nature. Taken together, these studies demonstrate the far-reaching positive impact of nature on all aspects of our physical, psychological, and emotional wellbeing.

I am not certain what exactly was causing all of Emily's symptoms, but I was certain that her hunger for nature was exacerbating them. Without my having to share my thoughts, Emily seemed clear about what she needed to do. Verbalizing her story made it clear to her that she was suffering from being trapped in an office building in Los Angeles, so far from all the nature that she loves. Emily proposed that perhaps she needed to take time to return home and focus on her health. I agreed and advised that we see each other a few more times before she leaves. In the interim I asked her to discontinue all her medications so that we could start from scratch. She was reluctant but acquiesced. I provided her dietary strategies and natural supplements for constipation as well as for nausea. I asked her to take several breaks during her workday to walk outside. I advised her to start a bedtime ritual, practice good sleep hygiene, and consider a cognitive behavioral program which has been proven to be more effective for insomnia than the sleep aids she had been prescribed. After I weaned her off the sleep aids, we tackled the anti-anxiety medication. By the time she returned to Utah, 6 weeks later, she was medication free. We met once more via telemedicine a month later. She had just returned from a hike with her father, and she was happy to report that thanks to "nature therapy," she felt better than she had in years. Her time away solidified the suspicion that her hunger for nature had made her ill. She took this information to realize that she could not return to Los Angeles or to her prior job. When she notified her boss, they offered her a position in Utah as the director of recreation, where she could spend her winters in the snow and the warm seasons hiking in the mountains among the nature that she loves.

Hungry
for Belonging

Johanna had moved to Los Angeles after completing her master's in psychology to start her clinical practice and her new life with her husband, James. Johanna and James were from Atlanta, where, she tells me, their lives had been very different. Having lived there all her life, Johanna left everything when she moved. She had friends in Atlanta, she had family in Atlanta, she had community in Atlanta, and then she had nothing.

"I am a total outsider!" she said as she threw her hands up in the air.

Johanna told me that, despite living in Los Angeles for 3 years, she had yet to find her *tribe*.

She also told me that she had gained 30 pounds since she moved.

"I don't understand it," she said. "I am always so hungry. And all I am hungry for is comfort food."

You are not hungry for comfort food, I wished to tell her. *You are hungry for belonging.*

It never occurred to me that I might not belong until we moved. In California, where I was born, everyone was different, so no one was really different. No one stood out. More importantly, I didn't stand out. It had never occurred to me that I wasn't *white* or *American*. After all, I *was* born over-looking the Torrey Pine Golf Course in the heart of La Jolla. What could be more gloriously American than that? But the circumstances of our move to Texas could not have more clearly demarcated my difference. We moved in the middle of the school year, and I entered the third-grade classroom that first morning after class had already begun. I walked into the deafening silence of a class of students working independently at their desks, all of whom looked up at me stone faced when I arrived. I immediately noticed the uniformly white skin of my classmates that contrasted with my darker olive complexion. One girl had her blonde hair pulled back into a thick braid, while another had it curled past her shoulders like Blair from *Facts of Life*. I resisted the urge to adjust the plastic rainbow headband that pushed my unruly short black hair off my face. I could not help but notice another girl who was leaning over the teacher's desk when I arrived, revealing the *Guess* label on the back pocket of her jeans. Not to mention her size. *She was so thin.* Thanks to the little white lie that had ushered me into kindergarten early, I was also a year younger than my classmates, in some instances more than a year, and somehow that seemed to show too. These kids appeared so much more sophisticated than I was.

Later that day, I walked past the row of lunch boxes. The Strawberry Shortcake lunch box in particular caught my attention. That one belonged to *Blair*. As I peered into my brown bag, I deliberated if I should pull out the contents. Mom had packed me an apple, an orange, and a homemade Persian "hamburger," wrapped in pita. The smell of meat and cumin seeped out of the bag. It was revolting, even to my familiar nose. I couldn't help noticing the neutral peanut butter and jelly sandwich wrapped neatly in wax paper, apple slices, and the snack pack of Oreos that came out of her box. How I envied those Oreos!

Even my Jewishness was a source of non-belonging, surprisingly, given that this was a *Jewish* school. But we were Sephardic Jews, unlike the other families, all of whom were Ashkenazi and from European decent. My family came from the Middle East. Our traditions, our food, and our culture were completely different from theirs, not to mention our appearance. As my peers would remind me, I looked more like Arafat's grandchild than a Jew. I was an outsider in every way imaginable, appearance, upbringing, and finances, and this knowing translated into a deep longing to belong.

My mother tried to help me find opportunities through sports and after-school activities. I participated in soccer, karate, and gymnastics and participated in dance. But it was not enough. The alienation at school overshadowed any potential for community that those classes could offer. I was hungry for acceptance, hungry for friendship, and hungry for belonging. But what I perceived was that I was hungry for food. I craved sweets, chocolate, cookies, and candy. But I did not find these things in my overly disciplined home. So, I settled for grilled cheese. My brother and I were left to our own devices until my parents came home from work. Our time was spent watching *Brady Bunch* re-runs until they arrived. I would make us grilled cheese sandwiches, sometimes one, sometimes two. As long as I was eating, I was not feeling. And I savored that respite.

The marriage between food and emotion is hardwired in our neurochemistry. In the many years of doing this work, rarely have I encountered a human whose emotions did not inform their eating. When we are happy, we eat. When we are sad, we eat. When we are longing, tired, and hopeless, we eat. The hormones that manage our hunger respond to food and nutrients, but they also respond to our emotions. In fact, our emotions literally hijack our hunger hormones. Research has shown that when animals are subjected to stress, they respond with an increase in the hormone ghrelin. Ghrelin is a hormone that is released from the stomach, signaling hunger to the brain. In normal physiology, an empty stomach will trigger the release of ghrelin, but studies show that stress will cause the release of ghrelin as well, triggering hunger and the desire to eat irrespective of food intake, resulting in weight gain.

But there are other ways in which food and hunger are connected in the brain. The limbic system is the part of our brain that is responsible for processing sensory input and emotional experiences such as pleasure and motivation. The structures of the limbic system are stimulated by alcohol, sex, drugs, and not surprisingly, by food. When we eat highly palatable foods such as sugar and fat, dopamine, a feel-good chemical messenger in the brain, or neurotransmitter, is released. Dopamine is responsible for the feeling of pleasure and satisfaction we experience when we eat. Dopamine boosts our mood and makes us feel happy, even euphoric, *in the moment*. Dopamine also interacts with other parts of our brains to coordinate a feeling of reward, reinforcing the positive feelings that arise from eating palatable foods and motivating us to do so repeatedly, thereby creating habit.

When we eat a chocolate chip cookie, for example, dopamine is released, and we feel pleasure. Dopamine stimulates the prefrontal cortex, the thinking part of the brain that helps us make the decision to eat more or to eat it again.

Yum, that cookie was good. I think I would like to eat more.

Dopamine also acts upon the hippocampus and amygdala, the parts of the brain that are responsible for emotional responses and the formation of memories. So, if your mother happened to make you fresh chocolate chip cookies when you were young to cheer you up when you were sad, dopamine would have signaled these structures to store that emotional memory.

My mom loves me. She made me chocolate chip cookies to make me feel better.

Months, years, even decades later, you will recall that sweet memory, whenever you come across the smell of fresh baked cookies, as a feeling of love, attention, and care. Finally, dopamine informs the nucleus accumbens, the part of the brain that executes the actions you contemplate.

I will walk to the pantry to get more cookies.

Or in my case, grilled cheese.

As if all of this were not enough, dopamine has yet another way of promoting the habitual intake of palatable foods. Over time, dopamine becomes less responsive to the food or foods we eat. Meaning that more food is required to trigger the release of dopamine and, therefore, the pleasurable effects of the food. So not only are we motivated to eat the chocolate cookie again, but we are required to eat more of it in order to get the emotional payoff. As palatable foods will result in pleasurable feelings, we become motivated to seek these foods in a repeated habitual way, particularly when there is emotional distress, so that we can reproduce feelings of pleasure. In these ways, food becomes synonymous with positive emotions and comfort.

"Comfort food," Johanna said to me as she settled back in her chair. As if just merely stating the words themselves signaled a sense of comfort and ease.

Comfort food did not get its name from nowhere. Based on all the mechanisms I described, comfort food does provide comfort, *in the moment*. But when the dopamine wears off, we are left unsatisfied and desiring more, which in essence is not comfort.

I challenged Johanna on this notion of comfort food. I asked her to think back to the last time she indulged in comfort food. Likely, the first few bites were enjoyable; they always are. But once that *wow* feeling wanes, we are left chasing it. In order to recapture that feeling, we are prompted to eat more *and more* and more. If we pay close attention to when we do indulge in comfort foods, we actually do not feel comfortable at all. Foods with excessive sugar, for example, result in a feeling of irritability and restlessness followed by sluggishness and fatigue. Food that is high in fat usually leaves us feeling tired, drained, even lethargic.

In reality, food that is completely the opposite of what we perceive as "comfort" is the food that in fact makes us feel comfort. When we eat unprocessed foods, fresh fruits and vegetables, lean protein, high quality carbohydrates, our bodies actually *feel* good, *comfortable*. Certain foods may represent comfort, but they do not actually *provide* comfort, not in the long run.

"Perhaps we should redefine comfort food?" I suggested.

The reality is that the comfort that Johanna was seeking was comfort from feeling isolated, from feeling alone and from feeling like she did not belong. It is not a surprise that she was turning to fried chicken and warm chocolate chip cookies or that I turned to grilled cheese. These foods stimulate dopamine in the same way emotional connection and heartfelt conversation and belonging stimulate dopamine. This is what Johanna was hungry for, not comfort food, but the comfort that is achieved from belonging. It took years before I would learn this for myself. Years before I would understand that my true hunger was a hunger for acceptance, for friendship, *for belonging.*

Johanna could see that her hunger for belonging had been displaced to food but was insistent to get this extra weight off right away. Her weight, in her mind, had become an additional barrier to social interaction given her discomfort around her body and weight gain. We created a plan that included diet, exercise, and medications for weight loss as well as a strategy to find her tribe here in LA. Perhaps she could join a professional group or a female networking club? I suggested. Maybe she would find like-minded peers at church or consider joining the choir as she had in Atlanta. Or maybe there were other avenues she had not yet pursued.

Johanna began the medications and slowly adopted some of the dietary changes although her cravings persisted. It was after months of working together that Johanna really began to embrace the suggestions I had made. Johanna reached out to the psychology department at Emory where she had earned her master's degree and learned that quite a few alumni were living in Los Angeles. In fact, they already had a professional networking group. Johanna connected with this group and met several like-minded peers.

She told me, in response to her successful weight loss, that her motivation was a desire to *look good* in anticipation of the social gatherings with this new group. Perhaps that was true. But perhaps with her hunger for belonging fulfilled, she no longer sought after the comfort of food.

HUNGRY
FOR SELF-ACCEPTANCE

MARILYN WAS 78 YEARS old the day she first walked into my office—78 years old and impeccable. Despite her advanced age, she lived an active and vibrant life. Marilyn was still working as a psychotherapist from the comfort of her own home, volunteering at a local animal shelter, where she had found her canine companion, and swam in her pool daily, a remnant of her college days as a competitive swimmer. When she first came to see me, Marilyn was suffering from severe arthritic pain in her hip and was hoping that with weight loss she could increase her mobility and resume walking long distances in anticipation of her trip to Europe. Over the course of 6 months, Marilyn lost the unwanted weight, traded in her walker for a cane, and headed with her friends on her European vacation. When Marilyn returned to my office 3 years later, a lot had changed, including financial loss and the death of her canine companion, all of which conspired in her weight regain.

"Are you still swimming?" I asked, remembering the awe with which I had first learned about her swimming career and her steadfast routine.

"Oh, I stopped..." she said as she shrugged her shoulders

"Why!" I said, taken aback by the abandonment of her beloved sport.

Marilyn explained that her financial circumstances had required her to rent out the spare room in her home to a young man. She was embarrassed to be seen by him in a bathing suit and had stopped swimming. I was shocked. Marilyn was so poised, so accomplished, so wise, how could she allow her sense of self to be robbed by a stranger nearly one third of her age?

Surprised as I was, I was also not so surprised. Self-acceptance and lack thereof is not dependent on age. Nor is it dependent on status, achievements, looks, or the many other external factors that we often confuse with our self-worth. Anyone can suffer from a lack of self-acceptance, and, truthfully, most people do.

We were still living in Dallas when I started high school. My high school was the opposite of the small private school I attended all throughout elementary and middle school. It was large, spirited, and diverse. But as I sat on the bleachers that day, all I could see was tall and thin.

I was right to not try out.

Despite my years of gymnastics and dance training, I did not belong on the cheerleading squad. Not that I did not have the skill, I did, but I did not have the look. By the time I was in high school, my weight had reached an all-time high. It did not help that now I had access to vending machines that could dispense every form of sugar and hydrogenated fat conceivable. As I watched the tryouts on the gymnasium floor, I alternated between deep longing and self-admonishment. *Tall and thin*, which I was not, was my justification for looking down from high up in the bleachers instead of cartwheeling down below. Then suddenly, in the midst of my ruminations, I saw Abby from math class twirling about. Abby was trying out for cheerleading? I was shocked...*and awestruck.*

"How could she?" I thought "She is fat like me!"

But she was not like me. Even from high up in the stands, I could feel her assuredness. It wasn't just confidence, it was ease, it was comfort in her own skin, it was a sense of self that was so powerful it was palpable, and it was so foreign to me. This sense I now know to be positive self-acceptance. Self-acceptance is defined as a "realistic appraisal that acknowledges all aspects of oneself, both strengths and weaknesses to formulate a positive self-impression." A person who has a high level of self-acceptance has a positive attitude toward themselves, is not overly self-critical, and does not wish to be someone else or something else. In this way, they are aware of their unique worth and accept who they are, as they are. Not surprisingly, positive self-acceptance is a key domain of happiness and wellbeing. In fact, psychologist Carol Ryff has found self-acceptance to be one of the six validated domains of wellbeing.

But what if you are innately self-critical, like me?

Back in the days that I marveled at people like Abby, I thought self-acceptance was an inherent god-given trait. Either you were born with it, or you were not. Perhaps it is true that some are blessed with a greater sense of self, but it is not true that this trait cannot be cultivated. Positive self-acceptance can be developed, but there are some key elements that must be understood. First, self-acceptance cannot be conditional. It is not self-accepting to say, "I will accept myself when I lose 20 pounds or when I get into law school or when I find my life partner." Self-acceptance requires us to meet ourselves where we are *at this very moment*. We are a culture of striving and achieving. Our appetite for wanting more, doing more, and being more is insatiable. But self-acceptance cannot be contingent on what we wish to achieve. This is not to say that we should not or cannot have goals or aspirations, only that our self-regard cannot be contingent upon them. When self-acceptance is conditional, then by definition, we are not self-accepting. Our desire for something more will always overshadow who we are in the present moment if we allow it.

Second, it is helpful to realize that self-acceptance is not a constant state of being. Rather, it fluctuates. We may embrace ourselves with self-acceptance in one moment only to doubt and criticize in another. In times of doubt, we may fear that we have lost our positive sense of self. But that is not the case. These sentiments, like all feelings, are fluid, and what appears lost can be recaptured. The awareness of its transience allows us to glide between self-acceptance and self-doubt without judgement, impunity, or fear. Understanding this ebb and flow allows us to accept its ephemeral nature, making its loss less meaningful and less likely to be integrated into a negative narrative.

Which brings us to the final point, which is that self-acceptance must be cultivated with intention and effort. Like a muscle that needs to be used in order to be strengthened, self-acceptance needs to be practiced and strengthened as well. The more we view ourselves through the lens of compassion and self-acceptance, the easier it is to recall this sentiment, to rebound from disheartened moments and to regain and remain in a state of positive self-acceptance. Building this muscle requires intention but is well worth the effort as it builds our capacity for this skill.

There are strategies that can help. In particular, a form of mindfulness by the name of *cognitive reappraisal* has been shown to be particularly useful in cultivating positive self-acceptance. This practice teaches us to disengage from negative thoughts and emotions by employing a detached attitude toward them. When we acknowledge negative thoughts but don't allow ourselves to get entangled with them, we allow them to pass more freely and to be replaced with more positive or benevolent thoughts and feelings. Cognitive reappraisal is effective in shifting our attitude towards negative emotions and beliefs. The ability to be nonjudgmental of our thoughts further boosts our ability to regulate our emotions and, in turn, to improve our mood. Studies show that of all the various types of mood regulation that can occur with mindfulness, cultivating self-acceptance is the most powerful at managing depressive symptoms and enhancing wellbeing. Finally, studies have shown that self-acceptance is an important pre-requisite for change and an important predictor to achieving our goals. The inability to accept ourselves as we are interferes with our ability to make change because we are more likely to sabotage ourselves by engaging with negative thoughts. However, positive self-acceptance allows for the necessary self-compassion and patience that fosters change.

I saw this playing out with Marilyn. While she had been able to lose weight with relative ease several years earlier, she struggled with it now. No sooner did she lose a few pounds before she would regain them again. She was so distressed about her weight and body that she could not allow herself to engage in the behaviors that could help, one of them being the return to her beloved sport. When I would suggest that she should consider swimming again, Marilyn always had an excuse. "Maybe when I lose 10 pounds," she said the last time I saw her.

Unfortunately for Marilyn, that time never came.

When we are unable to accept ourselves as we are, we get in our own way. When we are unable to accept ourselves as we are, we disempower ourselves and rob ourselves of the opportunity to do better, to evolve, and to grow. We also rob ourselves of the opportunity to do what gives us joy. Lack of self-acceptance kept Marilyn away from her beloved sport. My lack of self-acceptance kept me in the bleachers. Hunger for self-acceptance is also what led me to the vending machines, again and again, to engage in the very behaviors that caused the outcome I did not want. In retrospect, I wish I had developed positive self-acceptance at a younger age, like Abby had. While it would take a long time before I would learn self-acceptance for myself, I would learn. But not yet.

HUNGRY
FOR RITUAL

MORRIS WAS A GRADUATE student getting his PhD in neuroscience, working nights as a bartender to pay the bills, when he came to see me. His busy schedule over the 5 years earlier had resulted in weight gain that he was hoping to manage. The first time we met was right before the holidays. Between our overly restrictive diet mindset and our culture of over-consumption, the holidays are a hard time psychologically to "diet," but, ironically, it is also a time when some people start making changes in their diet and lifestyle to pre-empt the holidays, so to speak.

"It's not so much about the holidays," Morris said. "It's about sports. Thanksgiving is all about football in my family. And Christmas too. Football is our religion."

Morris was enthusiastic and embraced the plan we agreed upon and I started to see him regularly. He made changes to his diet, added in a few days of exercise, and even cut back on work by a few hours a week to allow for more downtime and sleep. But after the first few months, Morris began to skip his appointments. When he returned in late March, he had regained much of the weight he'd lost.

"Superbowl," he said apologetically. "I was doing great, but then the Superbowl happened, and once I fell off the wagon, I couldn't get back on."

But it wasn't just the Superbowl. Morris described a weekly ritual of gathering with the guys to watch sports and to eat. After a week of restraint, he binged on chicken wings, nachos, and beer. As I listened to Morris, I learned that it was less about the food and more about the sports. In fact, it wasn't wholly about the sports either, but more about the ritual of gathering with his brothers and dad. Our traditions and rituals, whether religious or otherwise, are inseparable from food and have been since the earliest civilizations. Ancient religions used food as an offering to the gods, and myths and legends imbued food with magical qualities. For example, *ambrosia* was a nectar of immortality for the Greeks, the Chinese believed dumplings could bring wealth and prosperity, and pomegranates granted fertility for the Persians.

It makes sense that food is a part of our sacred rituals. Food is sacred. It is holy, not only because food gives us sustenance and keeps us alive but also because of the way it connects us to each other and to our planet. Our food, be it plant or animal, is a living organism. At the beginning a seed is planted or an animal is born. Other living beings cultivate the growth of these living organisms. Farmers plow the field and harvest the fruit. Ranchers tend the herd and raise the cattle. Many labor to produce, pick, package and transport our food, which is then washed, measured, and prepared for our consumption and nourishment. Our food has crossed many hands before it reaches ours. When I consider this, I cannot view food as anything other than holy.

It's not surprising then that our religious traditions and rituals rely heavily on food: the Christmas meal, the Passover seder, Easter brunch, and Shabbat dinner, to name a few. And also, it is not surprising that many religions have laws that seek to guide us on what to eat and how to eat. Even for those of us who are not religious, these laws provide wisdom regarding how we use food to nourish our bodies. In fact, I wonder if I can help Morris relate these laws and traditions to his family rituals as well. After all, it's not the religion that makes the meal special; it is the ritual and what that food represents.

In Islamic law, *halal* and *haram* refer to the permitted and prohibited food and are based on considerations of the health benefit and the purity of food. Similarly, *kashrut* is the set of Jewish laws that guide food preparation and consumption. These laws are not arbitrary but crafted to encourage us to use food for health and wellbeing and also inspire us to use food in service of our bodies, in *reverence* of our bodies. This concept is first introduced in the story of Jacob and Esau in the book of Genesis. It is said that after working in the fields, Esau returned home hungry and found his brother Jacob cooking lentil stew. In his hunger for this meal, Esau impulsively traded his birthright as the first-born son, a position of leadership and inheritance, in exchange for a bowl of stew. Scholars describe this story as a cautionary tale against the use of food to satisfy desire. While we use food in a celebratory way, as part of our religious traditions and rituals, it is taught that we must still exercise restraint with our food, even in times of hunger. Can we then participate in the ceremonial aspect of food at these special occasions and still use restraint as a practice or as a form of ritual in and of itself?

Scholar Rabbi Shlomo Volbe writes that we must distinguish eating in response to hunger from eating out of desire. To distinguish between *needing* and *craving*, between sustenance and entertainment. In doing so, he encourages us to engage in a mindful eating practice. Mindfulness, in many ways, is at the core of these laws and traditions. For example, most religions have prayers that are recited before and after consuming a meal. This is not just an expression of gratitude but a practice of mindful eating. Prayer creates pause before and after the meal. Jewish law specifically urges us to create pause, to eat slowly and deliberately. Rabbi Natan of Breslov writes: "Be careful not to swallow your food in a hurry. Eat at a moderate pace, calmly and with the same table manners that you would show if an important guest were present. You should always eat in this manner, even when you are alone." Eating slowly allows us to acknowledge our hunger and also our fullness. But, more importantly, by eating slowly and savoring our food, we show respect toward our food and our bodies. If we engage in these practices deliberately, routinely, isn't this a form of ritual itself?

Anticipating a meal through pause is a form of savoring and can enhance the pleasure and enjoyment of food. There is also pleasure in satisfying *true hunger.* When we skip meals or ignore our hunger, it leads to a dysregulated response to purposeful physiologic cues. Allowing ourselves to get overly hungry makes it more difficult to feel sated, invariably resulting in eating in excess. Similarly, when we eat past our hunger, we feel overly full and uncomfortable, and when we are eating out of temptation rather than hunger, we may find that we don't have the expected enjoyment of the food. It is valuable to *feel* our hunger and to use it as a guide, both when to start eating and when to stop. And of course, when we take time to chew, we are able to appreciate all the sensory qualities that make food gratifying—taste, smell, and texture, aspects of food that are often ignored yet enhance the pleasure of our eating. That is savoring in the truest sense.

There is also ritual in the place that we reserve for food. Jewish law, for example, addresses the importance of sitting at a table as opposed to eating while standing or walking. Sitting for a meal at a specified place and without distraction inspires respect for the occasion of mealtime and a deference to the food we are consuming. This practice recognizes mealtime as a time for connection not only with our food but also with those with whom we can share a meal rather than being distracted from the experience by screens or our work as is commonly our present-day practice.

Interestingly, these ceremonial practices are shared by cultural traditions as well. According to author Amy Chavez, etiquette in the Meiji Period of the late 1800s dictated that one should not eat or drink while walking, and this practice has been integrated into present-day Japanese culture and law. In fact, the city of Kamakura enacted an ordinance in 2019 prohibiting walking and eating at the same time. On a family trip to Japan several years ago, I was amazed by the degree to which this practice was respected and preserved. No one could be found eating while walking in the streets.

Finally, we know that sitting while eating is vital for cultivating a healthy relationship with food. Sitting to a meal allows for presence, connection, and mindfulness. It also allows us to account for all the food that we are consuming. Studies show when asked, people underreport their caloric intake by up to 2000 calories daily. This is not because people withhold information intentionally, but it is more likely that they are not aware of everything they have eaten. We often start nibbling while we are looking for something to eat or while preparing a meal, or we clear off our child's plate at the end of the meal. Often, we don't have awareness of this. We grab a handful of nuts or candy, passing by our kitchen counter or someone's desk at home. It happens all the time. I encourage you to try an experiment: sit every time you consume even a morsel. You might recognize how often you eat something without being aware of eating it.

Family meals without distractions have also been shown in the medical literature as a way to cultivate healthy eating habits and to maintain healthy weights. "Food with family not technology," my children often hear me say. Family dinners have always been a priority in my household despite busy and divided schedules. Studies have also shown that sitting at the table and eating as a family is associated with reduced obesity and healthier weights in both the parents and children. Meal duration is important too. Children who engage with their families in a meal 20 minutes or longer four times a week are found to weigh significantly less than kids who leave the dinner table earlier than 20 minutes. And finally, studies have shown technology at mealtime is associated with greater food consumption, greater caloric intake, and excess weight in children. The intersection between our religious laws, cultural traditions, and science is a testament to the importance of these simple practices as a guide to living well.

I can understand Morris's hunger for ritual, the love for the dedicated time and place for sport and for family. I can also understand that it is difficult to separate food from this ritual given our cultural and religious norms. This overlap is purposeful, given the sanctity of food, and is not incongruent with preserving the sanctity of our bodies and our health. By implementing a personal ritual of mindfulness, pause, and attention to his food, Morris can achieve a sense of fulfillment of the ritual without neglecting his self-care, bringing balance to the sanctity of the occasion with the sanctity of his body and of the food itself. It is not so much about abstinence, but about attention, a mindful response to hunger and even to desire. We can choose to enjoy even our indulgences mindfully, and in that way make the food and the experience matter.

"Make it matter," I offered.

This language resonated with Morris. He continued his gatherings with the boys and implemented a ritual of mindfulness into his daily life as well as at these celebratory occasions. While he still feels he indulges at times, the concept of *make it matter* guides his decisions and allows him to make mindful choices that prevent him from indulging all the time or just because. In being mindful, Morris finds that his enjoyment of the food increases and his *over*indulgences becomes less. This shift is enough to initiate and sustain steady weight loss. The practice of mindfulness offers a new paradigm to satisfy his hunger for ritual.

Hungry
for Possibility

In retrospect I am not sure what was more intimidating about Janet, her commanding presence or her stern demeanor. Janet is 6 foot 2 inches with broad shoulders, evidence of her college days in pro volleyball. She barely smiled during our introduction, too busy managing her chewing gum perhaps, but her eyes met mine head on.

"I don't know why I am here," she said, more as a warning than an acknowledgement of regret. "I have tried everything, and I'm sure you have nothing new to offer.

"My husband and I live in the mountains; we hike 6 months out of the year and ski the other 6 months. I know how to eat and what to eat. So, I don't need you to tell me about exercise and a *healthy lifestyle*." She emphasized with air quotes.

"I have done everything. Diets, medications, shots, and nothing works, nothing will work, and I am the heaviest I have ever been in my life," she said, ripe with frustration. And with that she folded her arms and turned her attention back to her gum.

I can understand Janet's frustration, her anger even, and I can understand her disappointment. She is not alone in having traveled a winding, convoluted route. Most people do. In fact, we all do. The problem is not so much in the challenges we experience, but the expectation that it should be any different. I'm not sure who said that *it* (weight loss, relationships, our career, or anything in life, *really*) should be easy and straightforward, but that certainly is the predominant expectation. And this flawed expectation is the very thing that prevents us from truly engaging in this moment. True, Janet had been disappointed by past attempts, and at 260 pounds, she was the heaviest she had ever been, but failed past attempts, no matter how many, should not undermine this opportunity. People often are discouraged by past attempts. The burden of having not been successful or of knowing we once lost weight only to regain it keeps us from giving ourselves a chance for a different result. Whatever the experience, positive or negative, rumination on the past will taint us, impede our ability to start anew, and dissuade us from the *possibility* for something more.

As I mentioned, high school was an alternate universe for me compared to the small parochial school I had attended. I found myself among hundreds, thousands of kids. I marveled at the diversity: Asian, Black, Goth, punk, nerd. It gave me a feeling of hope and possibility. Possibility for a different experience, a new experience; I was certainly ready for something new. I was also ready to get the extra weight off once and for all. I had already tried so many diets. Diets I had read in books or heard about on TV, diets from magazines at the supermarket checkout stand and ones that were passed along from family or friends. I remember one diet that came on a frayed photocopy from some doctor's office, which allowed a menu of hotdogs, hard boiled eggs, and tomato slices for the first 3 days. I still marvel at how people come up with some of these things and more so how many of us fall for them.

I always started with the best of intentions. But even when they were sensible dietary plans, I couldn't fully commit. I was motivated but assumed that it would be an unsuccessful attempt, and that positioning undermined me from the start. I was so worn by the assumption that I could not succeed, that I *would not* succeed, that I never gave the opportunity a real chance and would sabotoge myself from the start. That's what past baggage does—it paralyzes us from progress.

There is a Buddhist concept called *Shoshin,* or *Beginner's mind,* that is incorporated in many Zen practices including meditation and martial arts. The idea is that one approaches every act as if doing it for the very first time. The attitude of a beginner's mind encompasses a childlike eagerness and enthusiasm. It is also free from judgement and expectation and therefore open-minded, open to whatever may arise. And finally, it is an attitude that recognizes the uniqueness of this moment. Past attempts are so heavy, filled with expectations, regret, judgment, and self-doubt that they invariably get in the way of a fresh start. In order to imagine the possibility of success, we need to free ourselves from old baggage; otherwise, they will interfere with the energy and effort that the present moment requires. A beginner's mind also honors the truth that we never fully achieve our final objective in a single attempt. Rather, it welcomes the process of molding and refinement that leads to true enduring progress. And thus, the beginner's mind honors process and *possibility.*

Past successes can be as discouraging as perceived failures. A prior weight-loss attempt which is perceived to have been faster, easier, or more successful will create resentment, a sort of envy of our past self. This comparison is just as harmful as a comparison to someone else. In the end, it is yet another self-defeating thought that will shake your faith in your ability to move forward. Regardless of whether positive or negative, that past attempt has *passed,* and reminiscing will impede you.

I encourage Janet to not allow her past successes or *perceived* failures (as I do not refer to past attempts as failures even if the desired outcome was not reached) to taint this moment. This moment is unique, I tell Janet. It offers hope and possibility. Janet is cynical but agrees to begin working together. When she returns to the office 2 weeks later, I am happy to see that despite her resistance she has decided to engage in the process. Admittedly, I am not yet convinced that her mindset will not sabotage her in the end but wish to acknowledge her engagement. Despite her skepticism she is here and has made changes that have already resulted in weight loss. Apparently, she is not convinced either as when I share my acknowledgement, she says, "So what? It's just water weight. It doesn't mean anything."

I was reminded that I cannot allow my own enthusiasm to override hers. This is a process, her process. She was right in that any strides will invariably be accompanied by setbacks. She experienced them before, and she would likely experience them again. That is part of the process too. But setbacks build resilience, making us better equipped to meet challenges and to persevere. Engagement in this process is not easy. It requires courage, bravery, and the audacity to imagine your potential. Believing in possibility is precisely what allows us to persist and to ultimately prevail. But we have to allow it. Janet had to allow it.

Janet returned again the following week and then again the week thereafter. Each time she demonstrated steady weight loss, and every time she dismissed her successes. I worried that her constant self-judgement would result in sabotage and wondered if her cynicism would finally prevail. How long could she continue to show up while her continuous narrative was one of imminent failure?

I wouldn't have to wonder long. On our last visit together, her weight loss had stalled. While she had lost 25 pounds, her weight remained stable over the course of a month, and she could not tolerate her weight being stagnant. She could not see it for what it was, just a pause. But a pause that allowed her past narrative to take hold and to overcome her hunger for possibility. Janet left the office seemingly more frustrated than when she first entered it, never to return.

While Janet had agreed, she had not engaged, at least not fully. Every visit was filled with judgement, with self-doubt, with the inability to let go of her past experiences. The possibility of a different outcome requires self-compassion and kindness that would have availed her if she had approached that moment with a beginner's mind. I understand the burden of past attempts and the disappointment of not achieving what we hope and expect ourselves to. But I also understand that every moment deserves the opportunity for a fresh start, one that is not tainted by the past. Every moment carries with it the landscape of that unique moment in time and, when met with the beginner's mindset, unlimited possibility and potential.

HUNGRY
FOR MOTIVATION

WHEN JOSH AND HIS father walked into my office, it took me a moment to figure out who in fact was the patient. His father walked in first, bold and brash, while Josh walked in behind him, reserved and unassuming. Why would he be there at all if not for himself? I thought. His father started talking before we even sat down.

"Let's get this guy ready for college," he said. "When I was his age, I was captain of the football team, I was always out with the guys or with a girlfriend. And I had lots of girlfriends," he added with a self-indulgent chuckle. "Let's get out there, have fun." He turned to Josh with a somewhat playful punch in the arm.

But Josh was not amused. When I spoke to him privately, Josh conveyed that he did not share the same interests as his father. He was not interested in football, in dating lots of girls, or in his dad's type of fun. Josh described himself as an introvert. While he had friends, they shared common interests like sci-fi fiction and coding. And while he didn't mind losing the "baby weight," as he called it, before he went to college, he wasn't motivated by football and girls. All of his life, Josh's father had tried to persuade him, pressure him, even bribe him to lose weight. He had tried everything from threatening his allowance to offering him a car. Despite his brashness, his father had a true desire to motivate Josh, but his attempts at motivation were not only unhelpful but also an obstacle. Motivation has to come from within. This I knew from my professional and personal experience. It was Josh's personal experience as well.

My family and I moved back to Los Angeles just weeks before mid-term exams my sophomore year of high school. Much like our move from LA to Dallas nearly a decade before, our move back was abrupt and untimely. Leaving mid-semester meant none of that year's work would translate over, and my upcoming exams at my new school would determine my mid-term grades.

We left so suddenly that when we arrived in LA, we did not yet have a place to live. Out of necessity, we moved in "temporarily" with my grandmother in her one-bedroom studio. My parents, my two younger brothers, my elderly grandmother, and I were all living in 850 square feet of space. Not to mention the new nanny we would hire to care for my 1-year-old brother so that my mom could return to work. The space was so small, it did not even allow for a desk, much less a separate area to study in. There was a dining table, but at night it was pushed aside, and the area converted into our sleeping quarters. We would spread blankets on the floor, where the five of us would sleep, leaving the single bedroom for my grandmother. I would lie awake waiting for the others to fall asleep so I could get up and resume my studies. But where, a flashlight under the blankets? I didn't think we had a flashlight. Maybe the bathroom? But the fanlight made too much noise. And then it occurred to me. I could use the kitchen!

Actually, it was a kitchenette, which was in close proximity to where everyone was sleeping, but I had a plan. After everyone fell asleep, I tiptoed into the kitchenette, cracked open the refrigerator door, and wedged my backside into the opening. The light inside the refrigerator lit up my books without disturbing my family. It strikes me that despite my eating habits at the time, I never ate while I was nestled inside that fridge, but I did find comfort there. Wedged inside the fridge, I would review chemistry equations, proof essays, and highlight textbooks until the late-night hours. It also strikes me that I never considered giving up. But I know why I didn't give up. Because my motivation to become a doctor was deep and enduring and nothing could shake that motivation.

Unlike Josh's father, my parents never mentioned my weight growing up, nor the weight gain that accelerated after our move back to Los Angeles. Perhaps they did not notice. Or perhaps they had bigger concerns—like finding a place for us to live and paying rent. Thinking back many years later, their silence bothered me. Maybe I wrongly believed that if they acknowledged my weight gain, it would have somehow motivated me. I now know that to be the furthest thing from the truth.

Motivation comes in two forms—intrinsic and extrinsic. Extrinsic motivation is one that is driven by external reward or recognition or by a desire to avoid punishment while intrinsic motivation comes from within. Josh's father's bribes and threats of losing his allowance are examples of extrinsic motivation. So are some of the other reasons my patients want to lose weight.

My husband or wife says I need to lose weight, for example.

Extrinsic motivation never works, at least not in the long run. Intrinsic motivation, on the other hand is different. When we are intrinsically motivated, we are energized by a deep conviction, a response to a personal need or desire. Because of this personal sense of fulfillment, we have an inherent drive to do the required work, and, therefore, we can do so with relative ease or at least with purpose. That is not to say that the work is not difficult, it just means that we can facilitate the doing of the work by aligning with a personal sense of mission and motivation. Inherent motivation is therefore connected to a deep sense of purpose, or to our deep-seated *why*. I had found that link between long hours wedged inside a refrigerator and my goals for my future, but I had not yet linked my weight to a deep-seated why; neither had Josh, and no amount of extrinsic motivation, positive or negative, from his father would change that.

Research has proven this to be the case. While intrinsic motivation is associated with greater weight loss, extrinsic motivation is detrimental. In one study, participants with higher intrinsic motivation were 3 times more likely to lose weight and were more likely 3 years later to have maintained their weight loss as compared to participants who did not report a strong intrinsic motivation. In other studies where financial incentives, in the workplace for example, were provided to encourage weight loss, these programs backfired and led to a reduction in intrinsic motivation and to greater weight gain when extrinsic incentives were removed, leading the researchers to hypothesize that extrinsic motivation led to "more myopic (or shortsided) unhealthy behavior than before the extrinsic incentives were introduced." We are unlikely to adopt or maintain behaviors that are extrinsically motivated, and adding external rewards will, in fact, make us even *less* motivated.

Suffice it to say, extrinsic motivation is ineffective. This was certainly the case for Josh as well as for me. I had the motivation to sit inside a refrigerator night after night and yet not have the motivation to make a change that felt so deeply important? I hated my body. But that is not motivation. Since that day when I was rebuked for my plate of food as a 6-year-old, the day that I defined my sense of self by comparing myself to the blonde in Guess jeans, the days of thumbing through *Teen* magazine as a child and *Vogue* as an adult, I had engaged in a punishing narrative which I used unsuccessfully to inspire change. That *was* extrinsic motivation. It was unclear to me then to what degree this negative narrative, this extrinsic motivator, prevented the change that I was so fervently seeking. And how in trying to motivate myself in this way I was, in fact, conspiring with the excess weight.

Commitment to a behavior, be it exercise or weight loss or studying wedged in a refrigerator, comes only when the action or behavior is fully aligned with your purpose, when the action has meaning that transcends superficial goals like looking a certain way or achieving acceptance even when that acceptance comes from a parent, as it did in Josh's case. Our inspiration must come from an earnest desire to achieve our personal best, not from admonishment or self-deprecation or the wish to appease others. Aligning with the desire to be fulfilled is much more powerful, effective, and *motivating* than an external source. The truth is that Josh was motivated to make changes prior to starting college but was held back only in his reluctance to appease his father, and, as the data showed, the extrinsic motivation served as negative motivator. I encouraged him to shift his focus from his father's wishes to his own. What motivated him to make these changes for himself?

We met only a few times before Josh left for college, but he felt confident on our last visit. Almost 5 years had passed when Josh returned home from college and reached out. He shared that he had lost over 30 pounds after he left home. He learned to cook for himself and joined a CrossFit community with whom he would work out regularly. But when he returned home, he began to revert to his old behaviors. He did not think much of it until it occurred to him that living at home and being exposed to his father's style of motivation had stripped him of his own. But this awareness was all that he needed to remind him of what he could accomplish when he followed his own internal voice, now that his hunger for motivation was filled.

HUNGRY
FOR UNDERSTANDING

"Just tell me what to do and I will do it," Tom said early in our conversation. "I have discipline."

Tom, a venture capitalist from Silicon Valley, had flown in on his personal plane to see me. He was well dressed with short hair and a close shave. I could not help but notice his upright posture as he sat in the chair before me, yellow notepad on which he documented my every word in hand. He continued to scribble even after I reassured him that all the information would be provided to him at the end of the visit. Everything about him screamed *discipline*, and I didn't doubt that he would do what I told him. Tom had already researched his options and was strictly interested in meal replacements.

"I don't want any choices. I know myself," he said, "and know that I cannot be trusted if I am given choices."

Meal replacements could fulfill Tom's need for structure and also address his fear that without discipline he cannot be trusted. But what I suspected was that what Tom really needed was grace. What Tom really needed was some understanding for himself.

The circumstances around our move back to LA were so tumultuous it seemed as though everything had been uprooted in our lives, and it had. There were the academic challenges I mentioned and the loss of our home and my personal space, the changes to my social life, and, of course, my father's work and the financial circumstances that prompted the move, which weighed heavily on him and on me.

We had planned that on moving day my dad and I would drive our car out to LA while my mother and two younger siblings would fly. As he placed the keys in the ignition, he sent me back into the house one last time to check for lights and unlocked doors. As I did my final walk through, I lingered in the kitchen by way of goodbye, fighting back my tears. I would not subject him to my sadness, nor my discontent. How could I when he seemed so broken? I turned off the lights and locked the front door before I returned to the car. He turned on the car without looking at me, but as he fastened his seatbelt, I could see that his eyes were teeming as well.

I started school the morning after we arrived in Los Angeles. By the end of the week, I was working for an orthodontist conveniently located between my grandmother's loft and my high school. I would walk there every day after school, and for $5 per hour, I would clean retainers, remove bands, and change brackets. After work I would walk home to have dinner with my family and start my studies. It was the same every day, like clockwork. Discipline came naturally to me. Discipline felt comfortable, and with the present circumstances as they were, discipline felt like loyalty to my father.

So, I became disciplined in my work, disciplined with my studies, and disciplined, frankly, in every way I knew how. The only thing I was not disciplined with was my diet. What I thought I needed was something structured and rigid. Like Tom, I, too, did not feel that I could be trusted with choice. So, I was thrilled when I came across *Slimfast*. I had seen commercials of skinny girls effortlessly replacing their meals with cans of this drink.

It seemed simple enough. Every morning I would stir a scoop of strawberry powder into a glass of milk and pack another scoop for lunch before walking to school. No sooner did I drink this disgusting concoction than I would already be thinking of food. I had discipline, but of course discipline goes only so far when it comes to our hungers.

I did not need more discipline, I needed understanding. Understanding for the child that had been uprooted from her teenage life just when things were starting to go right. Understanding for all my hard work and diligence that were now meaningless in light of an untimely move. Understanding for the deep loss my entire family was experiencing and understanding for my father's burden that I wished to carry, unable to tolerate his inability to grant himself grace. In light of all of this, Slimfast would not work, rigid diets would not work, and I would rebel against my attempt to discipline my diet as it was the only place in which rebellion felt safe.

Nearly 30 years later, I was back in my office with Tom, who was insisting on exclusively consuming meal replacements. I had learned since my own failed attempt that meal replacements were an effective strategy for weight loss when used in the right way. Ideally, meal replacements facilitate *easy* initial weight loss, which can be reassuring to the patient, who might be too overwhelmed to make the necessary changes at first and help them get past the hurdle of making more substantive changes. In fact, some studies have shown early weight loss to be the single most important predictor of long-term weight loss and maintenance. In one large clinical study, losing significant weight with the use of meal replacements in the first year was the biggest predictor of weight loss and maintenance 8 years later. High-protein meal replacements are also effective in preserving muscle mass, improving body composition, and facilitating greater fat loss in the long run.

Finally, their convenience makes them ideal to prevent skipped meals that can have unintended consequences. For example, consuming a high-protein nutritional bar might keep you from caving for a sugar-filled muffin when you pick up your morning coffee. Therefore, meal replacements offer an effective logistical strategy. But they are only a tool and will not, of course, address Tom's underlying hunger, as it did not mine.

Repeatedly, I attempt to share this with Tom, but he dismisses me. Tom proceeded with the use of meal replacements almost exclusively. He was losing weight swiftly and predictably but of course I was concerned about his inflexibility.

Just tell me what to do, he had once said, I have *discipline.*

Tom did have discipline. The discipline to complete his undergraduate degree from Stanford in 3 years. The discipline that drove him to secure millions in seed money for his first business venture while completing his MBA. Tom is disciplined and systematic in everything he does, which is in large part responsible for his success. But I worried that this discipline, this unyielding nature, and his inability to have understanding for himself would eventually undermine him.

Weight loss is often described in terms of discipline or, similarly, as willpower. But discipline is unyielding and intolerant of the inevitable setbacks that define this process. Willpower and discipline do not allow for the kindness and understanding needed to cultivate resilience and a sustainable path forward. When we engage in this practice with understanding, we are more likely to get up, dust ourselves off and resume our course when we do experience setbacks. We are more likely to resist shame, guilt, and self-condemnation when we get off-track, and, as a result, are less likely to self-sabotage and to give up. Discipline, on the other hand, is precisely what deters our ability to move forward and evolve.

Not surprisingly, Tom was meticulous about his appointments with me. He was seen at regular intervals; he was prompt and never skipped an appointment, until he did. After working with me for several months, he missed his first appointment. Two weeks later, he canceled another. Finally, he dropped off the schedule indefinitely. I cannot know for sure what happened, but I can imagine. His strategy failed him. He could no longer tolerate his overly disciplined approach and splurged or indulged or regained and was unable to see himself back. Tom's hunger for understanding went unmet, and without it he was unable to engage in this process no matter how disciplined he had been.

HUNGRY
TO HEAL

JOON IS NOTABLY ONE of my most affable patients. Every time I see him, he has a warm smile on his face. He is also one of my most overweight patients. At 5 foot 11 inches and over 450 pounds, Joon has a body mass index of 64, well over the cutoff for obesity and even super obesity. He has lost and regained over 100 pounds three times in his life, the last time following gastric bypass surgery, which resulted in the most significant weight loss but also in the most significant regain. In fact, Joon now weighs more now than he did before his surgery.

"It's always the same story," Joon said. "I know I can do it when I am committed. And when I'm committed, I lose weight quickly, but then I blow it, and gain it all back again."

I always ask my patients when they first began to notice weight gain. As a child? As an adult? And then try to determine if something in particular happened to them then. Sometimes an illness or a medication triggered the weight gain, but often it is triggered by something much deeper.

When I asked Joon this question, he answered without hesitation: "I was 7." Joon was so clear about when it all began that I continued my questioning.

"What happened to you then?"

He shrugged his shoulders, the conversation shifted, and we moved on.

Joon is easygoing and nice to work with. He asked if he could be seen every week for accountability, and I was happy to oblige. With every visit, he shared more about himself. His love of music, his special relationship with his nephew, and his love of cooking that is reminiscent of the time he spent with his grandmother, growing up. It was not until many months together that he shared that he and his sister lived with their grandmother from a young age. I wondered why but didn't ask.

Joon is as committed as he described. He showed up reliably for every visit, and the weight came off reliably as well. Within months of working together, Joon had lost over 40 pounds. We were able to discontinue metformin, which was prescribed for pre-diabetes, and he was able to wean off the CPAP machine for his obstructive sleep apnea. Even though he was still significantly overweight, his body was starting to heal. The body is so forgiving that way.

Then one day without any warning, Joon started to binge again. He was fixated on the potential weight gain. Even though he had not gained any weight, he hadn't lost weight that week and was very distressed. I was more interested in what might have prompted the bingeing. But he could not identify a trigger. He returned the next week to tell me that the bingeing had continued and that week it occurred nightly. He had gained 15 pounds. His discomfort was palpable. There is always so much shame around weight regain. He distracted us with jokes and banter. I smiled, but I didn't want to engage in the distractions.

"Joon, what happened?"

He let go of his upbeat façade for a moment and shrugged his shoulders as he always does when he is uncomfortable. He hesitated but then shared that his biological father died and triggered a return to old eating habits. The death of a loved one is traumatic in and of itself, but especially when it uncovers a deeper wound. Just as I thought this, Joon shared that he had been estranged from his father since childhood. The family had immigrated to the United States when Joon was a toddler. The transition was difficult for his father, who was unable to continue his work as an engineer. This resulted in depression and both physical and verbal abuse to the family. So much so that his father was taken into custody for a short time when Joon was 7. His mother was so distraught she suffered a nervous breakdown, and that is when Joon and his sister temporarily moved in with his grandmother.

Ah, so that's what happened.

Ultimately, his father moved back to Korea while the rest of the family stayed in the United States, never to see him again. The news of his father's death brought back the childhood trauma that he had not yet dealt with. I can't say that I can fully relate to Joon, I am hard pressed to say I experienced abuse, and I was never clinically obese, only obese in my head.

I am the oldest of three children. I have one brother who is 5 years younger, and another who is 14 years younger. We always tease the youngest that we broke Dad in for him. His experience was nothing like ours. He might disagree, but Dad had definitely chilled out by the time my youngest brother was born. I remember as a teenager telling my mom that yelling and shouting was verbal abuse. She looked at me with a mix of pity and amusement.

"*Boro, baba,*" she said. Which loosely translates into something like *girl, please.*

It's not like my parents were whacking us with shoes and rulers as they themselves experienced growing up in Iran. That kind of behavior was so commonplace back then that even the teachers engaged in it. My parents have shared stories, quite nonchalantly, of their teachers smacking their hands with rulers when their handwriting was subpar, mothers smacking an older sibling with a shoe for fighting with their younger siblings, and fathers whacking children's butts or worse when they misbehaved. So, they spoke loudly, so what? But *speaking loudly* is distressing to a child when it incites fear.

Many of my patients born in immigrant families, Latino patients, African patients, Asian patients, and Middle Eastern, have described similar experiences. For these families, even corporal punishment is not considered abuse, much less yelling and shouting. This is borne out in the scientific literature as well. According to the American Psychological Association, caretakers engage in the types of discipline that they experienced themselves, often because they and everyone they know were raised that way. Cultural norms and expectations vary widely in this regard, as do beliefs about what is considered appropriate discipline versus what is considered inappropriately harsh or even abusive.

Abuse in general is common in the United States and particularly common in the childhood histories of the overweight population. In fact, the connection between abuse and obesity is well documented in the medical literature. In a series of studies conducted by Dr. Vincent Felitti, childhood abuse has been associated with obesity in what we call a dose dependent manner, meaning the higher the number of traumatic events or types of abuse, the greater the risk of overweight and obesity. At the time, Dr. Felitti was the chief of the Department of Preventive Medicine at Kaiser Permanente San Diego, where he treated obesity. As he describes it, he discovered this link when he asked one of his patients "What happened to you then?" in reference to the time when she began to notice weight gain as a child.

Her disclosure of a childhood history of sexual abuse resulted in a hunch that Dr. Felitti went on to prove, that a connection existed between childhood abuse and trauma and obesity. In conjunction with the CDC, Dr. Felitti conducted a large-scale study in which he queried nearly 14,000 adults about adverse childhood experiences (ACE). ACE were defined as childhood histories of emotional or physical neglect or abuse, sexual abuse, exposure to violence, substance abuse, parental separation, or mental illness in or incarceration of a parent/caretaker. Nearly two thirds of the adults in this study reported at least one ACE. The presence of an adverse event in childhood increased the risk of developing obesity as an adult by 8% and the risk of severe obesity (roughly defined by 100 pounds of excess weight) by nearly 20%. The greater the number of ACEs present, the greater the risk of obesity such that individuals who had exposure to four or more experienced a 1.6 times increased risk of severe obesity. Finally, in a follow-up study of morbidly obese individuals who had lost more than 100 pounds, those who regained weight were significantly more likely to have a history of major childhood emotional trauma. Interestingly, some of these patients reported feeling "protected" by their obesity, less noticed because of it, and therefore safe from further harm by maintaining excess weight.

There have since been tens of thousands of studies of adverse childhood experiences in the medical literature. According to this data, over 60% of the US population has suffered at least one ACE and nearly 1 in 6 people have suffered four or more adverse childhood experiences. The presence of trauma in child-hood increases the risk of not only obesity but also metabolic disease, autoimmune disease, and certain cancers. Given the high prevalence of childhood trauma and abuse in the general population, it seems that an important question to uniformly ask is "What happened to you?" Unfortunately, anecdotal experi-ence and research demonstrate that patients' histories of abuse are rarely solicited by health care professionals.

Research has shown that merely 5 minutes of conversation around trauma is enough to reduce depression and anxiety in those who have suffered abuse, reaffirming that sharing the experience is essential and is the first step to integrating the history into a cohesive narrative that facilitates healing. Reaffirming, too, the human desire to heal.

I shared with Joon the data around childhood abuse and obesity and the subsequent health risks. I suggested that he start therapy in light of this event. Perhaps it would help address his history of weight cycling and his future health risk overall. The information seemed welcome to him and reassuring, and yet he was reluctant. I wonder if the connection between trauma and obesity was more widely known if it would serve to destigmatize obesity in the general population. A population that has already suffered so much indignity and shame.

What is even more fascinating is the mechanism by which trauma and obesity are associated. One might imagine that those with a history of childhood abuse are perhaps eating more because of difficult emotions. But the reality is much more complicated than that. Studies have shown that adverse childhood experiences result in epigenetic changes in the DNA of the affected individual. In these cases, traumatic experiences are the environmental factor that causes the epigenetic changes in the genome. Studies in adults who have suffered early childhood abuse demonstrate changes such as methylation in certain regions of their DNA that are not seen in non-abused adults. Methylation is a process in which genes can be turned on or off, thereby affecting the expression of the involved gene and therefore the characteristics that they code for. In fact, methylation is the primary way in which environmental factors can alter our genetics. One study comparing DNA specimens from children who had suffered abuse compared to children who had not revealed methylation of a wide range of genes responsible for neuropsychiatric disorders, cardiovascular disease, and obesity, as well as certain cancers, including lung, colorectal, prostatic, breast, colon, and ovarian cancer that were not present in unaffected adults who did not experience childhood abuse.

Joon listened intently, and I hoped he was encouraged to address his *true* hunger, his hunger to heal.

But then he canceled his next appointment and the one after that as well. Maybe I had said too much? Knowing the data, wasn't it my responsibility to ask and to encourage him to get help? And yet perhaps I offered too much too soon. I lost sleep over Joon that night and worried I would never see him again and that he would not get the help that he needed. Several months passed, and much to my surprise, Joon returned to my office.

He admitted that the feelings that surfaced following his father's death were too overwhelming, and he gave in to the desire to bury them with food. It is no accident that the individuals in Felitti's cohort felt "protected" by their weight. The shame that is perpetuated by hiding these stories perpetuates the need to hide behind layers of excess weight. But after a month of his own hiding, Joon decided he had suffered enough. I had learned about the therapeutic benefits of embodied practices such as yoga in addressing trauma. I asked Joon if he was interested and he was. He was also ready to start therapy. Slowly, Joon noticed the number of his binges per week dropped, and he began to drop weight again as well. It was the slowest weight loss he had ever experienced, but he noted that it was also the most transformative. The courage to share his story was precisely what Joon needed to satisfy his hunger, his hunger to heal.

HUNGRY
FOR SOVEREIGNTY

LIU WAS A YOUNG university professor who came to see me in hopes of addressing a 2-year history of steady weight gain. Liu is a highly accomplished child of an elite Chinese family. She had immigrated to the United States alone 2 years before to start her academic career. Liu made herself known among her colleagues for her aptitude for teaching and was ascending quickly up the academic ranks. She had also found a cohort of like-minded peers whom she socialized with. She seemed to have created a happy life for herself, except that she was not happy. In fact, she was depressed and felt plagued by what she thought was insurmountable weight gain. She had gained only 10 pounds, notable, but certainly not insurmountable.

Liu did come to the US for professional opportunity, but she came for another reason as well—to escape her parents. Liu had spent her entire life bending to her parents' will. Although she loved mathematics, they had made the decision for her to become a mathematician. They had also decided she should play the cello and whom she should marry. It was her parents who had arranged her engagement to the son of a prominent Chinese family, whom she not only did not love but also found *revolting!* Her decision to move to the US was under the guise of academic advancement but was in fact motivated by a desire to escape her arranged partner, to call off her engagement and begin a new life. Her decision to come to the US was motivated by her hunger for sovereignty.

While her parents still lived in China, they came for lengthy visits several times per year, during which they would stay with Liu. They were not happy about her decision to immigrate but were pacified by her ambition to advance academically. As such, they were still very much involved in her affairs and advised, if not dictated, many aspects of her life.

As happens to many people who move to the US, the change in lifestyle, processed foods, long work hours, and limited exercise had resulted in weight gain for Liu. But as often is the case, there was more to it than that. Liu was particularly concerned about her newly found obsession with sweets. She had never liked sweets, yet in the past few years, she had craved sugar in a way that felt irresistible.

"All I can think of is sugar!" she said.

"Between meals, after meals, and the worst? At night. Even if I convince myself to go to sleep without eating something sweet, I wake up and start searching my drawers, my pantry, and when I can't find anything, I end up running out to the gas station in my pajamas to buy chocolate. I feel so out of control." She ended nearly in tears.

This situation had become all the more difficult because her mother had very strong and negative opinions of her weight gain, and it had become yet one more thing she would berate Lui about, which of course drove her to consume more. Liu understood that the time spent with her parents further drove her hunger for sweets. Unfortunately, she did not understand why.

Lui had always been so responsive to her parents' wishes, so eager to please, that it never occurred to her that there could be a distinction between her thoughts and desires and theirs. They dictated not only what she did but also what she thought. What were *her* goals, her values, and her desires? When I asked Liu, she stared back at me blankly. She had been so tied to her parents' wishes that she didn't know her own. And when she was able to identify her own wishes, such as her desire not to marry the man her parents had chosen for her, her guilt kept her from expressing her discontent. Such objections also went against their cultural norms, in which parents were intimately involved in their children's affairs. Difficulty in creating separation from one's parents, family, and culture is so common in first-generation children of immigrants, particularly when families come from close-knit cultures like Liu's. I could certainly relate to Liu's dilemma, as this dynamic was very much a part of my Middle Eastern upbringing as well.

In many ways, my personal choices were aligned with what my parents wanted for me. But that only highlighted the times when they were not. My father was proud of my career choices while my mother had reservations, and they both had concerns about my choice of when and whom I would marry. Like Liu's, my cultural norms and parental expectations affected my personal decisions.

I don't know that I ever thought I would marry a Persian man. Given my background, it seemed obvious I would, but having spent my most formative years in Dallas, I had never been exposed to other Persian Americans until I moved back to Los Angeles. The largest community of explanted Persian Jews live in Los Angeles, and I became immediately met by peers who had similar upbringing and shared values. This provided me a deep sense of belonging that I yearned for. Within a few months of our move, a friend asked if I would join her for a weekend retreat with a local youth group. It was at this retreat just weeks before my 15th birthday when I met Bruce. He was a college boy, several years my senior. He was handsome. He wore his hair slightly long and slicked back, paired with a black leather jacket that definitely made him noticeable. When we happened to sit next to each other, we merely acknowledged each other at first, but then we started to talk. Within minutes, I would learn that we had everything in common. From our aspirations to pursue medicine to our love of Depeche Mode to our most recent reads, which included *Zen and the Art of Motorcycle Maintenance*. The more we spoke, the more we learned how much we had in common. The next morning, we were at a picnic with the same group when he predicted that we would be married one day. Almost 10 years to that day, we were. But getting to that day would not be so straightforward.

Despite our starry-eyed interaction, it wouldn't be until 2 years later when I was a senior in high school when we would start dating. My father was unhappy from the start. While he had left his home country as a young child and spent nearly his whole life in Europe and the United States, he was still an Iranian by blood and upheld the prominent cultural belief that boyfriends were unacceptable. Especially young, unestablished boyfriends. This relationship was child's play and in his mind would lead only to distractions and pre-marital infractions.

True, we were young, but we were also focused. We were not distracted, but rather motivated to pursue our shared goals. Our relationship spanned my high school graduation, my freshman year at UCLA the same year he was accepted as a transfer, donuts and coffee at *Kirkoff* coffee house, and late nights studying at the Biomedical Library. Despite our commitment to each other, I never pressed my father. I did not want to disobey him, nor did I want to displease him. As we grew together, we became more resolved to achieve our dreams together. Two years after we started dating, Bruce was accepted to medical school at Vanderbilt, what was the start to a long separation—one we would manage with nightly calls via a landline that bridged the 2,000 miles between us. In my desire to be obedient, I traveled to Vanderbilt only twice during those 4 years. Once as a day trip to interview at the medical school myself. I say *day trip* because my father forbade me to stay overnight. And the second time with my future mother-in-law and brother to watch Bruce graduate. Despite our years of commitment to each other, Bruce's commitment to school and my commitment to mine, despite the fact that I was old enough to vote, drink alcohol, and matriculate into my first year of medical school, my father was stuck in his disapproval, and I, stuck in my desire to please.

Despite what seemed at the time like an insurmountable obstacle, the solution was really quite simple. The solution was not to appease him but in fact just the opposite. The solution was to clarify my needs, to tease out my desire from those of others—even if that *other* was my father, whom I knew was operating from a place of concern, and to acknowledge that ultimately, he was ill-equipped to determine my path. Only then could I claim my sovereignty. Only then could I be free of my hunger.

I understood Liu and the fear/respect/regard that she held for her parents. But I also understood that the problem was not her parents, but her disregard for her own needs. When we compromise our needs for the sake of those around us—our parents, our spouses, our children, our bosses, or the many others who can fill this role—we undermine our independence, our authority, and create a hunger that aches to be satiated. Liu needed to clarify her own intentions and be unafraid to act upon them; only then could she too fulfill her hunger for sovereignty and build the life that she desired. Many years later, long after I was married and had children, I teasingly prodded my father about the grief he gave me and his now beloved son-in-law.

"How could I give my consent when you were so unsure?" he said.

In my desire to please, I not only failed to claim my sovereignty but also conveyed an uncertainty that perpetuated the very thing I sought to avoid.

My work with Liu consisted of strategies to help wean her off her sugar cravings and a practice of mindfulness to create awareness of the circumstances in which she would experience these unrelenting cravings. I asked her to try to understand what triggered her cravings, what were the precipitating circumstances, and, more importantly, what were the resulting thoughts and emotions. With mindfulness and journaling, it became clear to her that her desire to please her parents was to her own detriment and drove her to self-soothe with food.

Over the next several months, there was a dramatic change in Liu's disposition and outlook. What began as an existential crisis turned into a sea-change. As she became more intentional and self-assured, her life began to shift. Liu continued her academic post, but she made time for stillness and for play. She spent time in nature. She spent time in meditation. Liu was able to recognize that her desire to please her parents was at the expense of her own mental and physical wellbeing, and, armed with this knowledge, she could no longer continue the status quo. With time she gathered the strength to call off her engagement and to ask her parents to stay out of her affairs in general. She found, as I had, that once she claimed her sovereignty, her decisions were indisputable even by her parents. With this sense of agency, her parents' resistance softened. They were not in agreement, but at the same time they understood that they could no longer impose their will upon her.

Liu and I had long stopped talking about food and sweets. One day, Liu realized much to her surprise that her cravings for sweets had somehow just slipped away, and, much in the same, she noticed the weight slipped away as well.

HUNGRY
FOR MOVEMENT

MITCH WAS AN ENTERTAINMENT lawyer and senior partner who
came to see me to address years of weight gain. He told me that
his work was intense, and his activity used to match this intensity
until he was injured. Mitch had always been athletic and had
played football in high school and competitive wrestling in college.
While he chose not to pursue professional sports after college, he
continued an active lifestyle. Mitch played racquetball with co-
workers once a week and went cycling with friends every Sunday.
He was also an avid runner. Running was the only thing that
relieved him of the intensity of his work and allowed an escape
from his mind. But after a meniscal tear, Mitch had to stop running and never returned to his sport. In fact, he never returned
to any sport. Slowly, Mitch gained weight, and by the time he saw
me, he had reached a tipping point with the strain on his joints
making knee replacement imminent. As Mitch spoke, it was clear
that his weight gain was a result of not only a loss of activity but
also a spiritual loss that came from his loss of movement.

"Running was my religion," he had said.

I could understand that completely. Running had become a
religion for me too. A form of therapy, meditation, a way to clear
my head and bring about a sense of ease and peace of mind. But

I was not always such an enthusiast. Although I eventually ran a marathon, it is funny and somewhat embarrassing to remember how I started.

There was a time when I hated running. No. I abhorred running!

My painful memories begin with the fitness mile in high school. Back then, I could barely run a 14-minute mile; sometimes, it would take me 15 or 16 minutes to finish. How I managed to convince my PE coach to spare me this torment and allow me to grade his papers instead, I have no idea, other than to imagine that it was as much torture for him to watch me run as it was for me to run. Whatever the reason, I did not question it and happily graded papers until I graduated high school.

Many years later when I started medical school, I befriended a group of girls who would run after school. In the spirit of new friendships, I decided to join them. I can't say that I enjoyed the running at first, but I did enjoy the camaraderie. After some time, and I can't really remember why, I decided to start running on my own. I had always engaged in some form of exercise growing up, more because of a desire to be thin than for any other reason, but I developed the habit of regular exercise, nonetheless. What I did not expect was the pleasure I experienced with running. Despite the exertion, there was a certain contentment. In fact, the exertion *was* the contentment. Somehow, what I had perceived as torture many years prior became an embodied and tangible way to process my thoughts and emotions. Working through physical effort literally pulled my attention out of my head and into my body and in doing so relieved me of the worrying, thinking, and ruminating. I achieved mindful presence through the act of physical exertion, the breathlessness, the heaviness of my body, and inertia of my legs. Ultimately, the effort would give way to the flow of rhythmic striking of the pavement. Presence born out of movement. Unbeknownst to me at the time, this was my first lesson in mindfulness. With time the effect of this experience trickled out into my day-to-day. The feeling of calm and composure stayed with me and allowed me to be more tolerant and at ease.

In fact, vigorous exercise has been shown to reduce anxiety and enhance emotional resilience because of this physiologic stress. Increase in heart rate, body temperature and oxygen demand by the body, when navigated successfully, helps build emotional and psychological resilience.

So often my patients who were former athletes or have a history of being physically active in their youth have a similar experience to Mitch. These athletes appear to suffer a more dramatic weight gain as a result of their inactivity as compared to people who never exercised. As if their bodies get used to a certain degree of energy expenditure, and once they stop, the weight gain can be dramatic. But these patients also suffer in other ways. When robbed of their movement, they suffer a spiritual loss as well. They lose their tool for resilience and for tolerance and peace of mind. As a result, they seek other sources of comfort.

This was certainly the case for Mitch. After his injury, he became more confrontational at work and with his family. He became more easily flustered and angered. And he increasingly managed his unease with food and alcohol. He was not hungry for food; he was hungry for movement. I tried to offer him alternatives to his running: perhaps rowing would be less impactful on his knees, or maybe he could return to cycling. But he was not interested.

Mitch was diligent with the dietary changes and lost 30 pounds over the course of a year. After a few follow-up visits, his weight seemed stable, and we decided we could see each other less frequently. Mitch did not return until 2 years later. He had maintained his weight for the majority of that time until he hit a major life stressor. Since I had seen him, Mitch was involved in a fallout with his partners and had walked away from the law firm. The stress of this life shift pushed him into old habits, and he began to regain weight. Mitch understood that he was seeking an outlet for his stress and anxiety. Without movement, he was unable to process the intensity of his emotions. Without the intensity of movement, he was turning to food.

This time Mitch was more open to the strategies I offered. I myself had recently tried boxing and wondered if the exertion would match running for him, or even wrestling, which he had once loved. I shared this option as an alternative and convinced him to try a boxing class. The intensity of the boxing did remind him of his wrestling days and of the ways in which he had enjoyed the sport so much.

Mitch increased his participation and soon was boxing several times per week. He took notice of his mind and the fury of emotions he was experiencing, anger, frustration, and fear. Through the vigorous movement of boxing, he was able to work through the intensity of his emotions and achieve some relief. Mitch noticed when he focused on his body, his mind was clear. That feeling of ease was reminiscent of his running days. The more committed he became to his routine, the more committed he became to his food choices as well. This shift did not go unnoticed by him. He had understood his true hunger, his hunger for exertion, his hunger for movement, and the embodied experience that brought him ease and peace of mind.

Hungry
for Patience

Jan took out a wrinkled note from the bottom of her purse. It was faded, and I could barely make out the writing, but Jan told me it was a prescription.

"I was referred to see you over a year ago," she said. "But it took me a while to come. I just wanted to do it on my own."

I cannot say how many times I have heard this before, *doing it on my own*, as if it is a moral indictment to need help or to just want it.

"Well, I am glad you made it," I said with a smile.

But now that she was finally there, Jan felt a great sense of urgency.

Why now, I wished to know. Had something new happened? It turns out that nothing new had happened. In fact, Jan had been steadily gaining weight for years, over 20 years to be exact. Nonetheless, she was impatient.

Not that I didn't understand; I did. Once we become committed to this path, we are eager, but it is worth noting that these changes did not develop overnight, and they will not resolve overnight either.

"How much weight will I lose a week?" Jan wanted to know.

I am always reluctant to hand out numbers for several reasons. First, this magical number cannot be determined although people are made to believe that it can. It has been said that 1 pound of fat is equivalent to 3,500 calories, and, therefore, one can expect 1 pound of weight loss for every 3,500 calories not consumed. Calorically speaking, this conversion may be true, but it cannot be extrapolated, as it often is, that calorie restriction of 3,500 calories will result in 1 pound of weight loss. Based on that assumption, many people will suggest that a 500-calorie deficit a day results in 1 pound of weight loss per week or that a decrease of 100 calories per day will result in 35,000 calories or 10 pounds' weight loss in a year. But practically speaking, this is not true. This math does not consider the individual factors that are involved, not to mention the compensatory physiologic changes that occur in order to conserve energy when people begin to lose weight. Our bodies treat calories differently once we begin to lose weight. To compensate for the weight loss, our metabolism slows down and our bodies become more efficient at extracting fat from food among other physiologic tricks to keep us from losing weight. In short, this math does not take into account that we are talking about humans and not calorie chambers.

Patients often have unrealistic expectations in regard to not only how fast they wish to lose weight but also how much weight they expect to lose. Expectation management is a critical part of this process, and I am often in the precarious position of trying to manage expectations while providing encouragement and reassurance. People usually have a very specific weight goal. Often, that number represents their weight on their wedding day or their weight when they played college sports. They wish not only to lose weight quickly but also to lose a significant amount of weight, often a number they have not seen since the prime of their lives.

An interesting study assessed the expectations among a group of obese individuals enrolled in a weight loss program. Participants were asked to define what they considered as a goal weight loss as well as what they considered to be an acceptable and a disappointing degree of weight loss. The researchers learned that the goal was an average weight loss of 32%, meaning that the participants wished to lose nearly one third of their total body weights. The researchers also found on average a 37-pound weight loss would be considered "disappointing," and weight loss of 55 pounds would be considered merely as "acceptable." This study highlights the heavy burden of our expectations and an overall lack of patience with our bodies. Managing expectations when defining goals is important because often that is how we define our success. If we define success only in terms of these lofty and unattainable goals, such as losing *one third* of our total body weight, then we are likely not going to acknowledge smaller changes. Smaller changes that could be significant and life changing. Studies do show that as little as 5%-10% body weight loss results in significant cardiometabolic benefit—improvement in blood sugar, blood cholesterol, and blood pressure as well as a reduction in apnea and restoration of ovulation and fertility, among so many other health benefits. Moreover, without self-acknowledgment, we are less likely to achieve or maintain any degree of weight loss and, therefore, be further from our goals.

Unfortunately, our weight loss culture promotes unfair expectations with false and nonsensical claims. A recent internet search took me to a website that boasted "Lose 17 pounds in 4 weeks" (money back guaranteed). I wonder how they calculated such an odd number. But aside from its being a target that some may or may not achieve, the bigger problem is that it encourages the desire for expediency and distracts from the reality that this is a process, a process that requires time and patience if we are going to reach our goals in a durable way.

Impatience is one of the many reasons I wrestled with my weight as a young adult. I had unrealistic goals and expectations. I would weigh myself daily, sometimes several times a day. I'm not sure what I expected to see, but I was never satisfied with what I saw. How long can the psyche endure falling short? The answer is not long. I lacked patience with myself, patience with my body, and, invariably, that got in the way. My body hungered for patience, my psyche hungered for patience, but I was unable to grant myself that grace at the time.

Despite my reluctance to guarantee numbers, Jan agreed to proceed. I asked that she not weigh herself between visits. There is data that shows daily weighing is associated with more successful weight loss. It's a function of accountability and I advocate for it. But I also have found that, in some people, it results in a hyper-vigilance, a compulsiveness over the numbers that is demoralizing. I worried that this might be the case with Jan and that she would undermine her efforts in that way. When she returned the first week, she had lost 2 pounds.

"But it's only 2 pounds," she said.

Patience.

She returned the following week with another 2 pounds of weight loss and once again was frustrated.

"Two pounds a week," I said, "is 8 pounds a month, 24 pounds in 3 months, 50 pounds in 6 months! Even if we end up with a fraction of that, say 30 pounds, isn't that significant?"

She was momentarily reassured, but she blamed her body, her slow metabolism, her age as conspirators of the excess weight. I explained to her that when we are patient, our bodies do respond. I know this to be true. But week after week she dismissed her progress, and, ultimately, she did get in her own way. My reassurance was no rival to her impatience. Five weeks and 12 pounds later, Jan stopped coming in.

Unfortunately, that is not uncommon. While we hunger for patience, we do not allow it, and this mindset is demoralizing to the point of resignation. Expediency in weight loss is a false narrative that has been ingrained. We acknowledge that earning a degree takes time and patience, the growth of a business requires time and patience, a healthy relationship with a partner requires time and patience. But when it comes to our weight, we have an unrealistic attachment to what is expedient rather than what is practical and durable. And ultimately *this* derails us. When we are impatient with this process, we are destined to disappointment and self-sabotage.

HUNGRY
FOR CONNECTION

By ALL ACCOUNTS, LAURA was successful in every aspect of her life. She had lots of friends and an active social life. She was part of a book club and a hiking group and even made time to volunteer. Laura was successful in her profession and led a large marketing team. She was not yet married but dated frequently and told me that was "good enough for now." Her life was *full* as she had put it.

Which is why it was surprising to hear that she wanted a baby. Laura was not ready to settle down with a partner, but she wanted to have a child. During her medical evaluation, she learned that she had polycystic ovaries, or PCO, a diagnosis that affected her fertility as well as putting her at future metabolic risk. Weight loss is a recommended treatment for PCO because modest amounts of weight loss can restore ovulation and fertility. It may also reduce the risk of complications in the pregnancy and for the child. Over the course of 6 months, Laura successfully lost 20 pounds and then went on her way.

Just as it is not uncommon for patients to see me prior to pregnancy, it is not uncommon for them to return post-partum as Laura did. Particularly when in-vitro fertilization is involved because the treatments and hormones themselves contribute to weight gain. Laura's search for a donor and the grueling process of fertility treatments only heightened her longing to become a mother. But when she finally did become pregnant, she felt differently than what she expected. Laura didn't experience the immediate sense of connection that she had heard other mothers describe. On the contrary, she felt even more alone after the baby was born. Not only alone, but *disconnected*. Laura spent her days caring for her baby while continuing her work mostly from home. She felt inundated with the tasks and duties of motherhood. When I asked about her friends and family, whether they might be of help, she dismissed the question. She had returned to work part-time but felt her interactions with her colleagues intensified her sense of isolation. They couldn't relate to her, and she could no longer relate to them. She also did not feel connected to her friends. Laura's friend group consisted of single women who did not have the responsibilities of child care, and her friends with children were married, which offered a different dynamic than her experience of single parenting. And as for help from family, she did not feel it was necessary. It was her job to care for her child, she told me.

Laura came to see me not just because of the weight gain she experienced during pregnancy but, more concerning to her, because of the weight gain that she was experiencing since her pregnancy. Instead of losing weight post-partum, she was gaining weight, and over the 8 months since her baby was born, Laura had gained an additional 20 pounds.

"I never really feel hungry. But then again, no matter how much I eat, I never really feel full," she said, almost quizzically.

Laura found herself eating more food than she ever did before, a lot more food.

"I really don't ever feel full," she said again. "So, I keep eating."

Laura described that she could easily consume an entire pizza on her own or two entrees instead of one. When she was done, she would desire something sweet and then would pivot to something savory. Having already eaten "huge" portions, she was surprised by the fact that she could still eat a pint of ice cream or a reel of cookies. By my estimation, she was consuming upward of 6,000 calories at one time. And she did this several times per week.

Laura wrapped her cardigan around her body tightly as she spoke. I could tell she was uncomfortable with that admission, perhaps expecting to find me shocked or judgmental. But she found neither. Binge eating is the most common eating disorder, affecting up to 3% of the general population and even more in the overweight population that seeks weight loss. I tried to reassure her with a smile, and her arms loosened a bit.

"Do you ever eat like this when you are with your parents or friends?" I asked.

"Never," she said, seemingly horrified by my suggestion.

Eating alone is a hallmark of binge eating disorders, of which she had most of the diagnostic criteria, but that was not why I was asking. I was more interested in why she was so *alone.*

I suspected that her loneliness motivated her desire to have a child. Despite her *full* life, she was lonely. It strikes me that Laura described her disconnect to food much like she described the disconnect in her life. She had friends, family, a great job, a baby, but despite it all, she did not feel full, she did not feel connected. It is true that connection is not defined by the things and people around us. We can have spouses, children, friends, and family and yet feel so alone. I wondered if Laura had considered that having a baby could actually exacerbate her loneliness. This I knew firsthand.

My decision to get pregnant when I did seemed very logical. I had been married nearly 4 years, and while we were both still residents, I had several years before I would start my fellowship. Plenty of time, I thought, to have a baby. And just like that, I was pregnant. My sense of isolation was immediate. I felt alienated from my peers, many of whom were not even married yet, much less pregnant. Alienated from my friends outside of medicine, many of whom were starting families yet had opted to stay at home and were raising them under vastly different circumstances. Most poignantly, I felt alienated from myself. Getting pregnant immediately challenged my sense of self. The sense of whom I thought I should be.

In my fantasy, I would effortlessly balance my profession and motherhood. I would spend my days in the hospital then rush off to pick up my kids from school. I imagined presenting at academic meetings, then coaching soccer on weekends. I would wear lipstick by day then kick off my heels to cook homemade dinners at night. This external persona was immaculately planned, but my internal state—that was something I did not even know to consider. In fact, I was so driven by my external life, my doing and striving, that I was completely disconnected from my internal self. And my pregnancy had exposed this truth.

The tension manifested as a deep unrest within me. The moment I became pregnant, I began to question my long-held beliefs and aspirations. What if I really did not want it all? What if I no longer wanted to be a doctor? Maybe I had made a mistake in deciding to get pregnant then. These questions simmered in my consciousness, yet they were too painful to consider, too frightening to indulge. I could not fathom that I had gotten it wrong. Perhaps if I had allowed myself to acknowledge the unrest, I would not have felt so disconnected. All of my doings had been necessary to get me to this moment, but this moment required me to stop and listen to the rumblings inside me. But that was not my way.

Instead, I strived harder, indignant in my need to overcome my unrest. I could see Laura's tendency to do the same. I could see how pregnancy unraveled her delicate balance and exposed her need to pause and reconnect.

Despite my determination to be unchanged by pregnancy, I was changing. Despite my desire to ignore the restlessness, I became more restless. The more I shrugged it off, the more it stirred inside of me. The disregard to my changing experience, to my internal experience, enhanced my sense of isolation. The disconnect with my inner self, I could recognize later, only deepened my feelings of loneliness, a loneliness that intensified with the birth of my daughter.

I had only 10 weeks of maternity leave before my return to residency. Those 10 weeks sped by quickly. I passed my days nursing, pumping, cleaning, nursing, pumping, cleaning, and crying. Lots and lots of crying. My friends felt far off, my work and colleagues felt far off, my family, while physically near, felt far off, *everyone* felt far off. But the truth is I kept them far. I refused my mother's offer to return home with them after I gave birth so that I could benefit from her care and support. This would have made sense particularly since Bruce's call schedule left me alone many nights. I refused my mother-in-law's help with washing the baby when she came to visit. I even refused Bruce's insistence to change her diaper in the middle of the night when he was home. I felt deeply that it was my job to care for her and my job alone.

I never considered why I believed that I needed to do it alone. Certainly, this was not the tradition in which I was raised. In my tradition, mothers relied on community, and the community relied on them. My parents and grandparents did it differently. Multiple generations lived under the same roof, sharing the labor of the home. Childcare, cooking, cleaning, and feeding was done collectively. Children were raised in community by mothers and grandmothers, cousins, and extended family. Mothering was communal, so much so that mothers would literally give of *each other's milk.* My grandmother shares stories of how she laid the neighbors' child to her breast when the child's mother was ill and nursed her cousin's child when her milk had dwindled. This was not only a system of shared caretaking of the child, but shared caretaking of the mother as well. In the service of the child *and* the mother. This was true connection. How different this is from our paradigm, in which mothers are mothering alone.

I now realize that *alone* was of my own making. And it was complicated. On one level my loneliness was a function of my own obsession with independence. My strength, I believed, was directly proportional to my self-reliance. Needing or even wanting help was a sign of weakness. And accepting help was an admission that I could not give my daughter what she needed. As a working mother, I guarded against that admission with all my might. It took years for me to understand the value of shared caretaking the way that my grandmother had described. And to understand that acknowledging my needs was not a sign of weakness, but a show of strength.

But the truth is that I was disconnected from not only the people around me but also myself. I had spent so much energy focused on my studies, my goals, and my future, on what I *should* do and what I *should* feel, that I had no room for what I *did* feel. I had no room for what this pregnancy brought up for me—my need to slow down and reflect on the magnitude of this change in my life and to acknowledge the fear and self-doubt that arose because of it. My unwillingness to be with myself, to *connect* with myself, had gone unnoticed by me, but I could no longer tolerate that disconnect. This baby would not allow me that luxury.

Fortunately, Laura was already working with a therapist when I saw her. At my encouragement she hired a babysitter so that she could go out 1 night a week. An unusual assignment from a physician, but I had been given the same sage advice when I was struggling over how to give my daughter enough of me. The absurd assertion that I take more time away from her actually saved me. It reminded me that *relationship* needed to be nurtured. And not just with my child. My relationship with my husband needed to be nurtured. And perhaps most importantly, my relationship with myself needed to be nurtured. Allowing time away from her baby, I hoped, would allow Laura some space to find herself.

In trying to reconnect with her former book club, Laura stumbled into a writing group. She had never thought to write but was intrigued. The writing took the form of daily pages and introspections. Through writing, she explored her need for self-reliance and her fear of being in need. She acknowledged the weight of all the expectations, demands, and pressures she had placed on herself. Her writing allowed for a deeper understanding and compassion for herself. With time, Laura found her writing practice to become essential. It filled a deep void she did not even know she had, and this was both profoundly healing and transformative.

Through this group, Laura realized that even loneliness can be a shared experience. At first, she was reluctant, but every week Laura read her writings to the group as they did theirs. Sharing their vulnerabilities in this way allowed for a unique bond to form among these near strangers. Laura found herself not only opening up but also leaning in. She found that connection could be built from this place of shared humanity. And for Laura, the intimacy of this connection, this shared vulnerability, nourished her in a way she had never known. She also found that through this process, she was able to cultivate a greater understanding for herself. When we recognize our likeness, we give permission to delve into our own psyche in a non-judgmental and kind-hearted way. Engagement in this sort of self-discovery cultivates self-awareness and *connectedness*—with *ourselves*. Laura found over time that her way of life changed, her way of being changed, and without much struggle, Laura found that her way of eating changed as well. Laura told me that for the first time in a long time that she could feel hunger and feel fullness too. This awareness was everything and with her true hunger now realized, it no longer was masked by a hunger for food.

HUNGRY
FOR CONTROL

LORNA STARTED HER FAMILY at a young age and was heading into her 50s as an empty nester, with the last of her three children having just left home. Lorna was a dutiful mother, and despite her advanced education, she left a coveted clerkship with the US Court of Appeals when her first child was born. Her desire to be fully available to her children never allowed for the "right time" to go back, and so she dedicated all that energy to her family. Laura had spent her years as soccer coach, head-room parent, school fundraiser, and party planner. Having been so involved in her children's lives, the departure of her youngest was devastating. Lorna withdrew from time with friends and usual activities and from the little care that she had granted herself including morning walks with her neighbor.

It was with her husband's insistence that she take time for herself that Lorna came to see me. Lorna described weight gain that began during her childbearing years. While she had been able to return to her pre-partum weight, following the birth of her first two, Lorna never lost the 40 pounds she gained with her third pregnancy, and nearly 20 years later, she had gained an additional 30 pounds. Lorna was clear as to why, as she found herself eating compulsively all throughout the day. Short of this,

I did not learn much more about Lorna herself. Our first meeting left me with little information about her, but much about her children. Her eldest daughter, Jenny, had just had a baby of her own and was now returning to work after a yearlong maternity leave. The fact that she was not near Jenny, who lived out of state, was terribly distressing to Lorna.

"Who is going to help her manage the house? Who is going to help her raise that child now that she is going to work?" Lorna cried.

Is Jenny as distressed over her return to work as well? I wondered. *And how does Lorna's concern over her children relate to her compulsive eating?* I began to think that the two might be intricately connected. Our second visit together did not reveal much more information about Lorna either. That time, she was inconsolable about her middle child and only son, Jeffrey. Jeffrey was awaiting a job offer from an architectural firm in Chicago. Lorna was both worried that he would be hired, which would mean that he would not move back home to LA, *and* equally worried about him if he was not hired.

"He will just be crushed if he is rejected!" Lorna said as she sobbed into her tissue.

As it turned out, every visit brought a new dilemma about her children which Lorna agonized over. What if she cannot manage, what if he doesn't get married, *what if, what if...* Lorna seemed eternally anguished over the inability to manage her children's lives, to *control* the outcome of her children's lives. And it was clear that this anguish resulted in a lack of control in her eating. Control is an elusive notion. We seek to control our lives, but life consistently evades us. And when this is not met with acceptance, the result is a misplaced hunger.

I could understand Lorna's desire to control. I certainly have battled with my own desire for the same. When I became pregnant with my first child, I had settled into some comfort over my body.

Overall, I had settled into some comfort with myself in general. Tests and grades were mostly behind me. I had finished medical school and was thriving in a residency of my choice. After 4 years of separation, Bruce had returned and matched at his program of choice close by, and we were finally married and living under one roof. I had lost much of the excess weight of my childhood and young adulthood and with it the self-condemnation of my early days. I was at ease with my body. Not that I did not still obsess occasionally about the lumps and bumps. I did. But thoughts about my shape and size did not overtake my thoughts as they had when I was younger. My weight had been stable for years, and I was finally comfortable in my skin. But of course, pregnancy would upset that stability.

I was lucky in that my first pregnancy was easy, on my body that is; they all were easy on me in that way. But the truth is that I would not have had it otherwise. I did not have patience for a pregnant me. I could control my body and my pregnancy. I would not get slow; I would not get lazy. And I would not get *fat*. This last point I was certain of. I resolved to maintain a regimented diet and exercise routine. My breakfast was always the same, a cup of yogurt and a banana. If I did feel the slightest bit nauseous or craved a piece of bread, I would pretend not to notice. Not once did I indulge that desire. I continued to exercise religiously, going to the gym most nights after work, running on the treadmill far after the bounce of my growing belly made it uncomfortable to do so. And when doing hospital rounds, I insisted on taking the stairs, never the elevator. I even walked up the stairs to Labor and Delivery in between contractions when it was time to deliver.

But, naturally, my body changed, a change I did not have patience for. My legs filled, my waist grew, and my hips widened. I chastised myself with every change. I never considered pregnancy photos. In fact, I didn't even allow random photos, and those that have come into my possession have long been destroyed. I would like to say that by the third pregnancy, I thought less about weight gain, but maybe not. I had already had two healthy pregnancies and two healthy children, and each time, despite all my worry, I managed to return to my pre-pregnancy weight. I wish I could say that in the almost decade between my first and last pregnancy I let go of the desire to control. But that would have required a level of self-acceptance that was foreign to me at the time. As I think back, I want to apologize for my desire to control, my lack of faith in the body that cared for me and my babies so well. I took for granted what it meant to carry a baby. And for that I am sorry too.

But it wasn't only my weight I would control when I got pregnant.

People would ask me, "Are you nauseated?"

"No," I said adamantly.

"Are you tired?"

"No."

"Are you going to take time off?"

"No!"

I had a reputation for being a strong resident, and that reputation filled me with pride. I intended to maintain that reputation no matter what. If anything, pregnancy emboldened me to prove just how tough I could be. I took call, ran code-blues, worked long shifts, and remained sleep deprived. One night, while teaching a junior resident how to perform a lumbar puncture, I got poked after he drew out the needle. Our patient had AIDS, and we were doing a spinal tap to rule out meningitis. The nurse had asked me to reconsider doing the procedure, given his high viral load and the risk of a needle-stick injury given my pregnant state, but of course I refused. Another night, I was called into the CT suite for a code blue. It was only after the code was over and I noticed the technicians behind the glass shield that I realized I had exposed myself, and my baby, to the radiation of the CT scanner. It's not that I didn't care or that I did not worry, I did, but leaning into that worry would disrupt my illusion of control. I depended on that perception of myself, not only for how I wished to be seen, but for my own sense of security. My attempt at control lessened my fear and uncertainty over how my life was about to change.

Finally, I arrived at the end of my pregnancy. I had planned my maternity leave to start the day of my expected delivery so that I could spend the entirety of my limited time with my baby. By my 40th week, I was having contractions hourly, but I hadn't progressed.

"I could induce," my OB said, "or you can take the week off to rest and let your body progress on its own time."

The only way I would take a week off was after the baby was born. I would work until it was time. Only after another week of regular but ineffective contractions, of sleepless nights and awkward moments at work, I conceded. I woke up, blow-dried my hair, painted my nails, and made my way to labor and delivery. My impending motherhood had induced a different kind of control than Lorna's, but it was nonetheless motivated by the same desire to manipulate life according to my plan.

Our desire for control is motivated by a fear of uncertainty. The need for certainty is universal and hardwired in the brain as an evolutionary trait. Uncertainty is perceived by our brain as danger or a threat to our survival, akin to starvation or an attack from a predator. Therefore, uncertainty triggers the same sympathetic response as a life-threatening event. Control on the other hand gives us the notion (albeit false) that we can minimize uncertainty. But this is an illusion. Much of what we value most, our health, relationships, financial security, is subject to uncertainty. We are not in control of disease, natural disasters, economic downturn, and world events. Even the most resourceful individuals are met with adversity and uncertainty. Illness, loss of job, loss of income, deaths of loved ones, changes in relationships, and changes in work. Despite Lorna's wish to pave the way for her children and to protect them from adversity, it is not possible, and her attempts will leave her weary.

The antidote to control is its near cousin, environmental mastery. Unlike control, which is a futile defense mechanism, environmental mastery is a key determinant of psychological wellbeing. Environmental mastery is defined as the degree to which we feel that we have the resources and competency to regulate our environment and to cope with difficult circumstances. But there is an important distinction between mastery and *control*. *Mastery* does not mean *control*, but rather the fortitude to meet whatever challenge comes our way. It is knowing that we can withstand unexpected circumstances no matter how difficult. Inherent in mastery is the willingness to accept an outcome even when, *especially* when, it is not what we hoped for. Environmental mastery assumes a degree of surrender, knowing we cannot bend life's circumstances to our will and accepting that our best-laid plans can be circumvented by life's unexpected unfolding.

Lorna's desire to control her eating mirrors her preoccupation to control her children's lives. Her inability to make peace with food was symbolic of her inability to make peace with the fact that her children are no longer (or likely never were) under her control. I wondered if Lorna had ever considered that this acceptance might be empowering? Surrendering to what we cannot control allows us to direct our attention toward what we can control. We have choice in how we treat our bodies. We have choice in how we nourish ourselves, with food and by other means. We have choice in how we respond to life's circumstances. And in the end, that choice is so much more powerful than the notion of control.

I brought this up with Lorna during one of our conversations. But I wished to take her focus away from her weight. I suggested that since her children were grown, she could direct her energy elsewhere, maybe return to work or volunteer. Surely her legal background could be used to advocate for a cause she is passionate about. I also encouraged her to tune into her hunger. What does her hunger represent, a desire for food or for something else? Finally, I recommended that she consider seeing a therapist to help her with the transition in her life and the life of her family.

But she was fixated on her physiologic hunger. A hunger that was too much of a hurdle to overcome. She asked for an appetite suppressant to help. I understood but attempted to impress on her that long-term change would require that she address all her hunger in its entirety.

We started a medication, and Lorna began to lose weight. She was pleased until we reached a hurdle. Jeffrey did not get the job in Chicago but decided to stay there anyway instead of returning to Los Angeles. The grief and sense of loss was unbearable for Lorna. I recalled my own grief when I returned to work soon after the birth of my daughter. Once again, I offered her resources, including the list of therapists I had compiled over the years. She placed the paper on her lap as she sobbed into her tissue.

Finally, Lorna stopped crying. She adjusted her posture as she smoothed out the front of her skirt with her hands. Then without hesitation, Lorna stood up, thanked me for my time, and walked out of my office, leaving the list of resources on the chair behind her.

HUNGRY
FOR SLEEP

TANIA WAS A 38-YEAR-OLD force of nature. In addition to her day job as a medical assistant, she was finishing her master's in social work and volunteering at an adolescent resource center 2 nights per week. On top of it all, Tania had four children. As she shared her story, I marveled at her drive, her ambition, and her attitude. How did she do it all? And more importantly, *when did she sleep?*

As it turned out, she didn't. On the nights that she worked at the center, she made it home just in time to get her children off to school and to get to work at the hospital. She did sleep in on the weekends, but not nearly enough to compensate for her deficit. Over the 3 years since she started working nights, she had gained 40 pounds. Tania also noted that she had developed irresistible urges for fast food—something she knew she should not eat. While she had the tenacity to manage all her projects and responsibilities, she said managing the fast-food urges seemed impossible. She also was feeling uncharacteristically irritable and wondered if this was related to her poor food choices.

I think back to the times that I was sleep deprived. The all-nighters I spent studying for exams in college, call nights as a resident, and the many months of nursing my three kids, especially my son, who did not wean until long after his first birthday.

I experienced irresistible cravings in those times as well. In college, my craving was for donuts—in fact, I consumed a donut
every day of my first quarter in college. Funny enough, I lost 10
pounds that quarter because I was not eating much of anything
else. A perfect reminder that weight loss is not synonymous with
healthy eating. During my call nights as a medical resident, I
craved sour gummy licorice and always made sure to get a bag
from the hospital cafeteria before last call at midnight. And I
will never forget my always famished feeling while I was nursing
in the middle of the night. In those times, I craved pastries and
baked goods of any kind. Eating those forbidden snacks seemed
unavoidable and automatic.

This experience was shared by my classmates, my co-residents,
and is often discussed among sleep-deprived mothers. It is also an
experience that patients like Tania consistently report. We were
all eating to stay awake. And there is a reason this experience is
so universal; it's in our physiology.

Studies show that sleep deprivation is not only associated with
a higher risk of depression and anxiety but also increases our risk
for obesity and metabolic disease. In one study of over 60,000
nurses followed for over 16 years, women who slept 5 hours or less
per night had a 15% greater risk of becoming obese as compared
to good sleepers. Shorter sleepers were also more likely to gain
weight and on average weighed 30 pounds more than women who
got 7 hours of sleep per night.

The link between obesity and poor sleep is complicated and
is not just a matter of being awake longer and consuming more
food as one might suspect. Sleep deprivation, whether it is purposeful as in for shift-workers or organic as in insomnia or sleep
apnea, results in hormonal changes that promote hunger, insulin
resistance, and obesity. Studies have shown poor sleep results in

both greater hunger and greater cravings, specifically for foods that are higher in fat and in sugar.

Studies have shown that as little as 2 nights of sleep deprivation will increase the level of ghrelin, the gut hormone we have discussed that promotes hunger, and sleep deprivation also reduces leptin, the hormone released by fat cells which signals fullness or energy sufficiency. The study participants reported that these hormonal shifts promoted not only hunger and appetite but also greater cravings, in particular for foods that were high in fat and sugar.

We have moved toward de-prioritizing sleep to our detriment. Whether as a result of lack of boundaries around work and the need to bring our laptops into the bedroom or because of our desire to use our sleep time to unwind in other ways, such as by bingeing on Netflix or scrolling through social media, our sleep has suffered. In order to maximize our time and productivity, we have compromised our sleep. This was certainly the case for Tania. Not to mention for the large number of people who suffer from insomnia and other sleep disorders. Surveys show that more than one third of Americans get less than the minimum of 7 hours of sleep per night. Not only has sleep quantity decreased but also the quality of our sleep has been compromised. Sleep quality is affected by caffeine, alcohol, screen time, anxiety, and disruptive sleep disorders. Often, we may not perceive sleep disruption. For example, an apneic episode in sleep apnea will result in a micro-awakening that does not bring the person to a fully conscious arousal, but the negative impact on sleep, nonetheless, is the same.

I shared with Tania how the reduction of sleep time and sleep quality negatively affects health. After some discussion, Tania decided to defer her voluntary night position to later the following year after completing her course work allowing more time for sleep and the other lifestyle changes I had advised. Tania experienced an immediate increase in her energy level and her mood. She found the time and energy to start to exercise. She found herself to be less irritable and even noticed more meaningful interactions with her husband and her children. We discussed the option of medications for weight loss but never needed to use them. With adequate sleep, Tania's hunger is managed without anything else needed to suppress her appetite.

Sleep is integral to our nutrition and metabolic health, so much so that I often refer to sleep as a nutrient itself. I encourage sleep hygiene—reserving the bed for sleep only, preventing overstimulation with excessive activity or screens at night and creating a nighttime ritual that promotes sleep, such as reading, meditation, a warm bath or calming music, and I recommend limiting caffeine and alcohol. When that is insufficient, I advise that patients engage in cognitive behavioral therapy for sleep, or CBTi, which is the first-line treatment for insomnia and proven to be even more effective than pharmaceutical sleep aids.

I encourage my patients to aim for at least 7 hours per night, preferably 8. The ideal amount of sleep is 7-9 hours, depending on the individual. This will often incite a laugh or some other kind of protest—it seems so unlikely. But I remind them in addition to the metabolic benefits, there are benefits to memory, cognition, and concentration, and the time taken for sleep will likely pay dividends in terms of greater productivity and focus during the day. And of course, the benefits to mood, including reduced anxiety, irritability, and depression, are equally if not more important. As Tania came to learn, addressing her hunger for sleep enhanced her health and wellbeing—both mind and body.

Hungry
to Nurture

KAREN CAME TO SEE me soon after her divorce. As a single working mom, she was struggling to balance her work with her motherly duties, not to mention attempting to cope from the painful divorce that had left her reeling. Karen's weight had been relatively stable most of her adult life, but after her husband left her to marry the woman with whom he was having an affair, her weight skyrocketed. Karen and I had met only a handful of times before she confessed the timing was not right. Her wounds were too fresh, and she did not have the energy to engage in the life-changing process of reconciling her relationship with food.

I reconnected with Karen nearly 10 years later. Her daughter, by then 12, had her own struggles with food, and Karen sought me out to help with her daughter's weight. As an internist, I do not see pediatric patients, but I suggested that if she felt ready, I could help Karen herself, who could then implement changes in the home for the both of them. Change had to begin with Karen herself, I advised.

Our visits became a hybrid of conversations about Karen and her daughter. And often these conversations were one and the same. From the beginning, Karen complained that her daughter was the barrier to implementation of her own healthy diet. She insisted that she had to keep certain snacks in her home on account of her daughter but was unable to resist the temptation herself. When I suggested that the snacks and sweets were not in either of their best interests she would object.

"She is just a kid!" Karen said, throwing her hands in the air as if incredulous that I could not understand. "If I try and just feed her broccoli, then she won't eat anything at all. And what about her friends? We have to have something in the house for when she has friends over."

There was no end to Karen's reasoning for why she had to keep unhealthy food in her house, yet she was not willing to acknowledge that they were both steadily gaining weight as a result. It was not until her daughter's 13th birthday that I understood how deeply interconnected the relationship with her daughter and the struggle around food was in her home. Karen had been planning her daughter's birthday party for months, and despite her efforts in making this the most memorable one ever, she seemed to consistently fall short. Karen's daughter was unrelentingly dissatisfied with her mother and challenged her every move. Why couldn't they go *out* for dinner, her daughter complained. When Karen shared that she could not accommodate all her guests in their car, her daughter protested. Why couldn't they rent a bus to transport the friends she hoped to invite? Why couldn't they celebrate with ice-cream cake *and* donuts? Why couldn't they buy a waffle maker for breakfast the morning after the sleepover? In the end Karen conceded to all her daughter's demands, most of which revolved around food.

In fact, it struck me that all of Karen's discord with her daughter revolved around food and was the reason that Karen could not set boundaries around food at home. This became even more evident after the party was over. Karen, who had attributed a 1-week weight gain of 5 pounds to all the leftover "junk" from the party on her previous visit, had returned 2 weeks later with an additional 5-pound gain. Why was the *junk* still in the house, I wondered? We had discussed that the availability of this food in the home was triggering both of them to consume it in excess, and now that the party was over, it might be best to get the leftovers out of the house. We even strategized offering the cakes to the nanny or donating the packaged items because wasting food was an additional concern. And more importantly, we discussed how to engage her daughter in this process to empower her to be an advocate in her own health.

Karen's response was an outpouring of emotion and grief over her husband's infidelity, his abandonment, and, most painful, his neglect of his fatherly duties toward their daughter. This was a topic that Karen had been unwilling to broach before then and one that had been a driver, in my mind, of her inability to set boundaries with her daughter.

"He is never around," she sobbed. "He never participates in any of her activities, he never makes it to her school plays, to the holiday shows, her teacher conferences. And now that he has another child, he barely even calls, not even for her birthday!

"Everything has been taken away from her. I can't take this away from her too!" Karen said of the food that she was supplying her daughter. It became clear that Karen was using food as a comfort for not only herself but also her daughter. Karen was hungry to soothe her daughter, to nourish her, to *nurture* her. But of course, food used in this way would not soothe, nourish, *or* nurture her, not in the long run at least. It only taught her to use substances for comfort. It taught her to rely on external sources of comfort. It taught her to seek solace from outside herself instead of teaching her the valuable tool of comforting from within. And yet I could understand as a mother how food was used to nourish not only the body but also the psyche, the mind, and the soul.

For me, food was ingrained culturally as a form of nurture, as it is for many of us, and unbeknownst to me, I adopted this wholeheartedly as a mother. My 10-week maternity leave whizzed by faster than I could imagine, and I returned to my residency utterly bereft. I had transitioned from the pregnant resident who stubbornly marched up and down stairs, who ran code-blues from the insides of a radiology suite, who ignored contractions so that I could keep working, to a mother so distraught over the thought of leaving her newborn, I wished never to return. The conflict between my long-held desire to become a doctor and the desire to nurture my newborn raged against each other. But of course, I would have to return. I eased back into work with a rotation at the free clinic near the homeless shelter in downtown LA. While the population was challenging, the short hours were appealing. But even a 20-hour work week was too demanding at the time. The guilt of returning to work and the separation from her felt unbearable and fueled my obsession to feed her.

I was determined from the start that I would exclusively breast feed. As a physician, I knew the benefits of breast-feeding, but I was motivated more by my refusal to share my maternal duties with another caretaker whenever possible. My guilt over having to leave my child to someone else's care made me resolute in being her only source of nourishment. I had planned in obsessive and intricate detail how I would achieve this goal despite my erratic resident schedule. Before she was born, I purchased a hospital-grade breast pump and a 5-cubic-foot freezer that I used exclusively for the storage of breast milk. I was hopeful that by starting to pump prematurely, I could amass a stockpile of milk. The lactation nurse had advised otherwise; becoming an *over-producer* of milk was not as favorable in her mind as it was in mine.

In my mission to build up my milk-stores for my impending return to work, I started pumping the day I was released from the hospital. I marked and arranged the small baggies of milk by amount and by date. I indicated with colored markers a morning batch from evening batch, knowing that milk consistency changed over the course of the day to meet the child's needs. Each baggie was stored systematically for future use. By the time I returned to work, 10 weeks later, I had amassed so much milk that I had to pile textbooks on top of the freezer lid to keep it closed.

Back at the free clinic, I broke away to the storage closet where I could pump. Amongst shelves of cleaning supplies, I lined the dirty floor with paper towels before setting down my travel pump. Pressing my back against the lockless door, I fastened the small plastic membranes to the adaptors and then screwed the adaptors to the milk bottles. Then I connected the whole contraption to my chest and to the breast pump with clear tubing that I had meticulously cleaned and steamed the night before. Turning up the machine as high as it would go, I bypassed the recommended "let-down mode." It wouldn't be long before my male attending would notice my absence. As the machine tugged at my breast, I felt the familiar queasiness that arose just before the let-down reflex of milk. This feeling always filled me with sorrow.

Was this what was referred to as the dysphoric milk ejection reflex—the emotional drop that some woman felt right before the let-down—or did I just miss my daughter? What was she doing right then? Did she know that her mother was not there? Was she dysphoric too?

As the milk streamed into the bottles, I watched my tears spill onto the floor.

Sheereh ghareh nadeh beh bahchat. "Don't give your child anguished milk," I could hear my mom say, as if milk could somehow transmit my anguish.

As the stream of milk dwindled down to a trickle, I disassembled myself and packed up my pump quickly before placing it under the table filled with patient charts waiting for my attention.

By the time I started my intensive care rotation 3 weeks later, I had become proficient at my pumping practice, but time was becoming an even scarcer commodity. Sometimes 10-12 hours would pass before I would make it to the call room nestled in the center of the ICU to pump. Amid the dings and bells of ventilators, I would pull out the pieces and assemble the pump quickly, hoping to be done before my pager went off. Often, I was successful, but just as often, I was not. One particular night, I was so engorged from the wait that I pumped four 6-ounce bottles of milk in one sitting. I was thrilled. *This will be at least 2 days of milk*, I thought. Just as I was placing the last bottle down, I was startled by the sound of my pager and knocked over all six bottles like dominos. I froze, horrified as I watched the milk pour out all over the floor.

They say a mother's milk is *liquid gold*. This could have not been more true for me then. Despite my diligence, my absence from her was affecting my milk supply. I had taken to hoppy beer, fenugreek, lactation teas and other medieval remedies to increase my milk supply, but by the time she was 6 months old, I was really struggling. To make matters worse, she had come to prefer the bottle over the breast, which impacted not only my milk production but also our time together. It was on one of those post-call days when it became clear that my desire to nourish her was impairing my ability to nurture her.

After a long 36-hour shift, I rushed into our apartment to feed her. I had alerted our nanny to keep her hungry for my arrival, but when I sat down to feed her, she showed no interest.

"Come on," I said with frustration.

But to no avail. She refused to nurse. I panicked. I had purposefully skipped my last pumping session to ensure that I would have enough for her. If I did not pump then, it would almost certainly affect my supply. I set her down in her bouncer and stormed into my room to pump. When I returned 20 minutes later, without a drop of milk to show for it, I found my daughter being bottle fed by the nanny. I can still recall the feeling of rejection that seared through me at the time.

The interconnection between nourishment and nurturance is ingrained in our physiology. Oxytocin, is released in the mother's circulation even before a child is born, stimulating labor and the production of breast milk. The first cry of the newborn triggers oxytocin as does the child's suckling, allowing for continued milk production until the child is satisfied. During breastfeeding, this *love hormone*, as it is often referred to, is released not only in the mother's circulation but also in the bloodstream and brain of the child, fostering feelings of love, generosity, empathy, and secure attachment between the pair. In fact, oxytocin is associated with emotional and social connection throughout life. The dual role of oxytocin underscores that care and nurturance are just as essential to human survival as food and sustenance. But it also underscores why we, as mothers, might conflate the two.

I now realize that I had equated my desire to nurture with an intention to nourish. And while they are not inseparable, they are not equivalent. To nourish is not the same as to nurture. And to nurture, we must do more than just nourish. To nurture is to provide attention, love, and care. But it also demands boundaries and restraint. Nurturing requires fostering resilience and flexibility and providing safety and security so that our children become adept and agile and tolerant of the injuries that they will invariably experience, as we all invariably do. It was a distinction I failed to recognize those many years ago and a distinction Karen had failed to recognize as well. I would have to learn that to nurture beyond the limited way in which I defined it, and so would Karen.

When we first met, Karen had not been ready for the deep emotional work of coming to terms with her hunger, and she was not ready 10 years later when she returned. While her awareness that she was using food to soothe herself and her child was a beginning, it was not enough. I suggested, once again, that she and her daughter, for whom she had frequently solicited my advice, would benefit from attending to and finally healing the wounds of her husband's infidelity and neglect. While she had wished for guidance, I imagine that this was not the guidance she was hoping for as I would not see Karen in the office again.

HUNGRY
TO GRIEVE

I HAVE SHARED BEFORE that people often cry in my office. I keep a double box of tissues at the corner of my desk. Their sadness always stirs up emotion in me, but sometimes their sadness is almost too difficult to witness. Rose was one of those patients. We had been working together for some years. In fact, I had first met her prior to her gastric bypass surgery. She had seen me for a medical clearance and for preoperative weight loss, then went on to have surgery. Rose was diligent after surgery and lost and maintained her healthy weight for nearly 7 years before she came back to see me.

Rose had shared certain details of her personal life. She was a nun who led spiritual retreats for women who suffered domestic violence and other traumas. I never asked why she had chosen this work, but I was so intrigued by it that I remember this detail now many years later. On the day she returned, we greeted each other warmly. Of course I remembered her. I am not great with names, but I never forget a face. After some brief catching up, I asked her about the circumstances of her weight regain. No sooner did I ask this question before she began to cry so severely that her body shook.

After what felt like a long time, Rose regained enough composure to speak again. "I wasn't always a nun," she said. "I was married once. Paul and I met in college and were married 6 months later. We both wanted a big family. Soon after we married, Bella was born." Rose's body heaved with sorrow.

"Bella was perfect," she said after a long pause. "She was playful and precocious. Paul was infatuated with her." She looked up at me with a smile. "The two of them were in love."

Rose looked back down and continued her story. When Bella was 2 years old, Rose was giving Bella her nightly bath when she noticed that she was out of bath soap. Being alone in the house, she ran downstairs to grab a new bottle from the laundry room. When she returned after what felt like just an instant, she found her perfect Bella had drowned.

The details of this incident were lost as Rose was sobbing so heavily that her words were unintelligible, but her sentiment was not. Rose went on to share that her marriage to Paul could not withstand the stress of this tragedy, and soon after they were divorced. It was because of this that Rose decided to join the convent and lost contact with Paul. The year before she came to see me, Paul's sister, who had remained an ally to Rose, reached out to share that Paul had died of cancer. The news unearthed this old trauma and sent Rose into an emotional spiral. She had resumed old and maladaptive eating patterns. Her sleep was negatively affected, and she began to suffer nightmares like she had when Bella first died. Rose became preoccupied once again with guilt and the circumstances of Bella's death. And now this grief was complicated by Paul's death. It was only through her spiritual work that she was able to acknowledge her hunger to grieve. But despite the 40 years and the new life she had created for herself, it was clear that Rose had not fully grieved this loss, or maybe loss of this caliber is never fully grieved.

When I returned to work from maternity leave, I had yet to experience true grief, although I would with time. But I felt grief. I felt immense and perhaps exaggerated grief over leaving my child to someone else's care. But when I was at work, I was fully immersed. Fully immersed in the work and in the grief of others. My work demanded a high degree of presence, particularly my work in the ICU. By then I was a senior resident, the most senior person in house for the round-the-clock care of the sickest patients. I finalized clinical decisions, signed off on medical orders and determined who would be given the limited beds in the ICU. The patients were sick, often unconscious and hooked up to ventilators, monitors, and IVs. And though they were usually under my care for no more than days, these patients stayed with me. Patients like Shayna. I will never forget Shayna, nor will I forget her mother.

"Hi, sugar." Shayna's mother beamed as I walked into their room.

Shayna was 26 and paraplegic. Her immobilized state set her up for frequent infections and hospitalizations, but her young body always made it through. According to her mother, her stays were short, and her recoveries complete. Despite the unfortunate circumstances, it was clear that Shayna's mother valued her life. Her mother attended to her dutifully and did not seem bothered by her role as a full-time caregiver. Given her daughter's history, she had no reason to believe that this hospital stay would be any different from her others, nor that 24 hours later her daughter would be gone. I will never forget her heart-wrenching screams when I told her that Shayna had died.

I will also never forget Angie, the 98-year-old grandmother with heart failure who died quietly on a morphine drip while her family waited patiently and lovingly in her room. Nor Meredith, who came in obtunded and yellow from the cancer that had invaded her liver. I still remember her manicured nails, evidence that just days before her hospital admission, she was a regular woman doing regular things. I became immersed in these stories and in their grief. While I had not personally been confronted with grief in the ways I had witnessed those nights in the ICU, I knew that grief cannot be ignored, no matter how much time has passed.

Rose knew it too. Her work as a spiritual leader had taught her that. But in a way, Rose was skirting along the edges of her own grief by helping others process theirs. And now she had to contend with her own hunger to grieve. Grief is not completed on a timetable. Most people are familiar with the stages of grief as defined by psychiatrist Elizabeth Kubler-Ross in her 1969 book, *On Death and Dying*, and may experience some or all of these stages, which include denial, anger, bargaining, depression, and acceptance. But even as Dr. Ross later explained, these stages do not occur in a particular sequence or at a particular time, and grief more often than not lingers or reappears.

Grief is a normal response to loss, and difficult emotions are expected. However, when these emotions are not fully processed or when the distress is so severe or prolonged that it interferes with the ability to engage in life in a meaningful way, as is the case in complicated grief, that is when additional help is warranted. Loss and grief can also result in emotional eating, substance abuse and obesity. While Rose described her own spiritual work as therapeutic, she had never addressed her own grief in therapy. Pharmacotherapy with antidepressants is often prescribed in complicated grief, but they have not been shown to be effective. However, psychotherapy that is focused on bereavement has been shown to resolve complications of grief and provide mechanisms to adapt to loss. While Rose had come to see me for weight loss, she agreed that might prove too arduous then. My goal was to just stem the tide of weight gain that began with the news of Paul's death rather than make weight loss a primary focus. Invariably, addressing her grief would be the only way to address her hunger. Rose began to work with a therapist who specialized in traumatic loss and bereavement. She also continued her own spiritual practices in the convent where she lived. Inevitably, it would be a long process. I imagined a never-ending process. But reckoning with her hunger to grieve allowed her to reckon with her hunger for food as well. And in the end, Rose realized, that was one and the same.

HUNGRY
FOR LEGACY

THERE IS SOMETHING VERY comforting about Suzanne. I sensed it the moment she walked into the office. She has a warm smile and a warm presence. I was not surprised when she described herself as a "good ol' southern mama." I could almost imagine her in the kitchen, cooking up apple pie. In fact, that was how she often passed her time. Suzanne came from a long line of cooking mamas. As the matriarch in a large Southern family, caretaking was her profession, she told me, and it began in the kitchen. Suzanne's life was marked by big family gatherings, Easter, Thanksgiving, and Christmas, and by smaller ones in between, summertime barbecues and Sunday brunches. There was no end to the opportunities to gather her family around food. Cooking was her inheritance. As a young girl, she would partake in the ceremoniousness of cooking with her mother, grandmother, even her great grandmother, she told me. For Suzanne, cooking was the way she experienced her family's legacy, and that's the reason she could not separate the two. I could understand Suzanne's sentiment. Food is interwoven into my family's fabric as well. And I have carried this legacy from my childhood and into motherhood.

"Mmmm, it smells like Shabbat," my kids say as they arrive home Fridays after school. I bask in their delight. I don't cook

Persian food every night, but I do cook it every Shabbat. I would not say that I grew up religious short of Friday nights. Shabbat *was* religion. In the Jewish tradition, Shabbat is a time dedicated to rest, to shutting off from the busy-ness of the workweek. In our family, Shabbat is a time for togetherness, for family, and for food. From a young age, it was impressed on me that nothing could excuse me from being home on Friday night—no football game, no birthday party, no outings. Friday was for family.

I am still in awe of the flurry of activity that surrounded my mother's arrival from work Friday afternoons. She came home with bags filled with fresh vegetables and herbs, burlap sacks of rice, poultry and meat wrapped in brown paper and coarse string, satchels of spice and a sundry of other items. I can still remember the red rings marching up her arm where the bags had hung. Before the groceries were packed away, the water was already boiling, ready for cups of long-grain rice. Later, she sieved this rice at the precise moment when the grains were soft on the outside yet still hard at their core. I would not know the art of this timing until many years later. Even a second's delay would spoil the pillowing of this soft rice—this is what made our rice so unique. In two separate pots, she caramelized onions to translucence with stew meat and turmeric. Later, she would mix tomatoes, eggplant, and French-cut green beans in one pot and, in another, hand-chopped herbs, including parsley and fenugreek. In a large stainless-steel bowl, my mother would wash watercress, mint, basil, and other herbs, their bright green leaves contrasting the red radishes that bobbed among them. Finely chopped carrots were sautéed with cinnamon and pistachio then mixed with rice. Hours later my mom would flip this tall pot of rice in one swift movement, revealing a golden saffron crust. The air was at once filled with the sound of sizzling, the clang of pots and pans, and an orchestra of smells of food. How my mother managed to pull this off week after week, month after month, and year after year, I do not know, but I do know it was an act of love.

I was never a cook. I made it through the first 2 years of med school (my first experience living away from home) eating toaster chicken—that's what I called the Costco chicken tenders I would buy in bulk and cook in my toaster oven. I made some attempt at cooking after I was married, but it wasn't until I had my own kids that I yearned to continue the legacy of food and family. I was hungry for this tradition and hungry to pass it on to my children. Standing in my own kitchen, caramelizing onions, soaking herbs, sautéing meat and spice, I feel tethered to my past. Cooking these dishes feels like a calling, an inheritance in a very tangible way, as if it has literally been passed down in my DNA. I was never taught how to prepare authentic Persian food per se, but I grew up witnessing the preparation, the labor of it. When it was my turn, I drew my instruction from an intuitive place, a deep knowing that felt innate.

Science has revealed that cooking, in fact, is a biologic trait, an adaptation that was essential to human survival and evolutionary change. Prior to the advent of cooking, humans consumed a raw-food diet that was inadequate to meet the caloric needs of the hunter-gatherer. Plant foods were too fiber-rich and meat too tough to extract all the nutrients and calories when consumed raw. Cooking, which popped up across many parts of the world contemporaneously, allowed for food to become softer and more digestible, allowing for quicker and easier release of nutrients. This access to nutrients and calories resulted in anatomic changes in humans, including refining our dentition and our digestive tract. More importantly, access to more nutrients in our food allowed for greater brain capacity and ultimately led to the evolution of the human species.

If it is true that cooking literally contributed to our evolution, it is not far-fetched to imagine that how we cook and what we cook is also ingrained in our DNA, an imprint that is passed on generationally from grandmother to grandchild. As I cook, I am aware of my place in this succession, of my kinship with my mother and grandmother, my ancestors, and my past. I recognize that for me and for Suzanne, this is not just about food, this is about family and connection, love and belonging, and this is exactly the sentiment that Suzanne expressed as well. But it is how we reconcile this inheritance with the equally important birthright of wellbeing. It is our birthright to live well, of sound body and sound mind.

Our initial blood work showed that Suzanne had diabetes, just as her mother and grandmother had. She recalled memories of her mother's failing health, an inheritance she did not wish to receive. Our work together was challenging as unraveling deeply ingrained behaviors is. But I asked Suzanne, can you honor your heritage, your legacy, while also honoring your desire to be well? Can you relish in this deeply meaningful legacy of food while being mindful that food is also fuel? That it must nourish not only the soul but also the body? That excess will be cause to inherit a different legacy of illness and disability that you do not need to inherit?

Suzanne was skeptical, but I knew that it was possible. With intention and persistence, with purpose and resilience, Suzanne could attend to her hunger in a way that nourishes her body and soul, and so we began our work together that would span over a decade and to this day.

Hungry
for Approval

JUDY WAS THE LONG-TIME executive assistant to a well-known music agent. She loved her boss and was dedicated to her work, yet years of living at the whim of his demanding schedule and even more demanding disposition had resulted in self-neglect and weight gain. Judy felt the timing was not right to start working with me but then admitted that the timing was never right. She had been contemplating this for years and finally decided she had to take time off for herself.

Judy and I worked together for 6 months, during which time she lost less than 5 pounds. Not that she was not committed—despite her difficult schedule and the lack of weight loss, she continued to make an effort to see me. But her schedule was never her own, and she would frequently have to reschedule or push back visits because of an audition or a concert and once because she had to escort her boss on a last-minute trip to Las Vegas to ensure a perfect birthday celebration for his wife.

Judy did love her job, but it was clear that she had outgrown it. She knew she could no longer remain at the beck and call of her boss at the expense of her own wellbeing, yet she had trouble moving on. It was not a financial concern as she and her husband had planned well, it was not a fear of being unemployed as she had a side business that could have easily occupied her time, and it was not even loyalty per se, but there was a hunger I could not identify. Nor could she.

Judy had started that job over 20 years before. At the time she was in a difficult place in life, following the divorce of her first husband. It was an emotionally abusive relationship in which she never felt valued. Her then husband made constant demands and had unending complaints about everything from her clothing to her work salary and her parenting style. Judy described the relationship as an unending desire to please and seek approval—an approval she never received. She took this desire into her work as an unyielding devotion to her boss, a desire to please and a hunger for approval. She basked in his approval when it was offered and sought it out when it was not. Much had changed since then, but not this.

Hungry for approval.

My return to residency after the birth of my first child was physically and emotionally taxing, but what was most taxing was the upcoming fellowship that loomed over my head. I had actually fantasized once about becoming a surgeon. Trauma and gynecologic oncology intrigued me. But I felt that these paths were too long and arduous, so I decided to pursue internal medicine so that I had the option to subspecialize or not. There were so many options—cardiology, oncology, critical care, but what I was most interested in as a medical student was gastroenterology. I'm not quite sure why. I do recall a lecture by a female gastroenterologist. She was so intelligent and articulate as she stood there in her red lipstick, high heels, and white coat. While I cannot imagine I made a life-defining decision based on that one moment, it did stay with me. I do know that I was drawn to the field itself because it allowed for a combination of consultation and procedure. Procedures meant you could do something, meaning you could fix something. And back in those days, I thought meaningful work as a physician involved fixing people. But part of me was interested in the field because it was so sought after. At the time GI was one of the most, if not *the* most, esteemed fellowships in medicine, and I was motivated by the challenge and the recognition and approval among my peers if I should be accepted into such a coveted fellowship.

Matching would be even more challenging because I applied only in the local area, which narrowed my options to just a few hospitals. Bruce and I had already spent sufficient time apart, and I wasn't willing to do that again, especially since I became a mother. My mentors tried to prepare me for the likelihood that I would not be accepted, considering that I had limited myself so, and I had prepared myself for that possibility too. But then I was. I was actually accepted to two programs before I withdrew from the rest, and I was elated. Because I was still an intern when I was informed, I had 2 years before I would start my fellowship. And then I had an idea: I could have a baby! I had time. If I got pregnant, like immediately, I could spend a whole year with this baby before I would have to start the fellowship. And so I did get pregnant immediately, and that is when my dread began.

The moment I learned I was pregnant, I felt the rumblings in the pit of my stomach. Something would have to change. Finishing my residency was hard enough, but the fellowship would be a nightmare. Three more years of training. Three more years of being on call, of pagers, of emergencies. Three more years of my time not belonging to me. But then again, how could I quit? This is what I had always wanted, or so I thought. It is what I loved, and the fact that I was one of the four out of thousands of applicants who had applied and been accepted at this particular hospital didn't make the decision any easier. The thought of quitting was heretical, if not psychotic. I tormented myself with the decision about what to do. If I am honest with myself now, I know that my struggle was not because of my love for gastroenterology or the belief that I would not be happy practicing any other area of medicine. My torment came from wanting the prestige that came with the fellowship more than the fellowship itself. My torment came from a hunger for approval. A hunger I felt I could only fulfill through the praise and approval of others.

Then one day something happened. Ellia was 4 months old while I was on my ICU rotation, the rotation of spilled milk. I was post-call, and we were heading home. It was dark by the time I picked her up from my parents, and holiday shopping season made traffic unusually difficult even for Los Angeles. The drive was hideous. Stop and go, stop and go. She began to cry and within seconds was wailing. Nothing comforted her. I stopped, I nursed, changed her diaper, her clothes, burped her, tried to bottle feed her, but she wanted none of it, and nothing would appease her. Given that Bruce and I were splitting the commute between Los Angles and Irvine at the time, it was never a quick drive, but that trip took hours. She cried and I cried the entire way home. When we did finally arrive, we were both completely depleted. Only after I had gotten her to bed did I realize that Bruce was not even coming home that night. I had completely forgotten that he was on call and I could have stayed with Ellia in LA instead of making the arduous trip home and back again to work in the morning. It was just too much to bear. I crawled into bed in my day-old scrubs and cried myself to sleep.

I woke up the next morning clear-headed. This was a mandate I could no longer refuse. On the face of it, this was a reckoning between motherhood and my profession, but in reality, it was a reckoning of my hunger, my hunger for approval. Ellia cried for her needs, but she also cried for mine. I was someone's daughter too.

On some level my desire for approval also felt like a mandate. My father had relentlessly pursued education all of his life. At age 11, his father sent him to a boarding school in England for what he thought would be better educational opportunities than what was available to him in Iran. My father never returned to his homeland, opting instead to move to the United States to continue his undergraduate studies. He did not have the money to fly and tells me he gathered just enough funds to travel with a single suitcase by ship. He can still recall his exuberance his first day of school at UCLA. My father's path led him from one institution to another, collecting degrees and post-doctoral positions, including a master's and a doctorate and another doctorate, before he settled as professor at the University of California, San Diego, School of Medicine, where I would be born and also where I would return to earn my medical degree, a coincidence that is not lost on me. Despite his many accomplishments, he did not achieve the medical degree that his father had wished for him. He had sacrificed everything for his education, for *his* hunger for approval. I don't believe that my decision to pursue medicine was born out of his hunger, but I do wonder if my hunger for approval was. An expression of empathy, even loyalty to him.

I have always been aware of my desire for approval and have been unapologetic about it. It served me well, I thought, made me appreciated by friends and family, respected by peers and my superiors. I was considered helpful and reliable, but it did come at a cost. Seeking outside approval is tiresome and unproductive because it is a chase that, in the end, is unfulfilling. Our psyche seeks and even needs outside validation, but only by gaining inner approval can we truly satisfy this hunger. Without approval for ourselves, everything else will fall short.

After years lacking awareness, Judy came to realize her pursuit of approval and the ways in which it was informing her life, her relationships, and her health. Her relationship with her boss came to a head on her husband's 55th birthday. She had planned a weekend get-away for the two of them to celebrate. She had even opted to go three weeks before her husband's actual birthday in order to accommodate her boss's schedule. But when the time arrived for their excursion, Judy was dragged into an urgent project causing her to miss their flights. Her husband protested but she did not heed his protests, and he left without her, leaving her to work in their apartment alone. This moment was painful but also enlightening as it brought about an awareness to what she had been doing for years, and this awareness changed everything. She finally quit her job with a renewed sense of freedom which had a rippling affect in other aspects of her life. Judy noticed the relationships that were no longer serving her. The habits that were no longer serving her and narratives that were no longer serving her. It is with this renewed spirit that she returned, a spirit that allowed her to approach her weight loss goals and her wellbeing with conviction and success.

HUNGRY
FOR EASE

MARK WALKED INTO MY office, BlackBerry in hand. "Fuck," he
said, as his phone dinged.

And this is how our relationship began.

Mark is a defense lawyer, a good one. He had been hailed as
the best negotiator in town and was awarded and punished with
a case load that kept him in the office 7 days a week. His lunches
were often rushed at his desk or at meetings with clients. Either way
he was making poor choices. His dinners were not much better.
Mark had been married 12 years and had three young children.
He usually arrived home after 8 pm, after the kids had already
eaten and often when they were already in bed. He described his
home life as *fucking chaos*. And because his wife did not cook, he
settled on the kids' left-over pizza, or cheese and crackers, and a
few cocktails, usually two and sometimes three, "to take the edge
off." He would continue his workday in the bedroom, where after
reading memos and responding to emails, he would settle into
a fitful sleep, rarely sleeping through the night. He was back on
his BlackBerry by 5 am.

Not surprisingly, Mark was resistant to change. When I suggested that he make different food choices at work, he told me
that he couldn't risk his clients' seeing him eat like a *fucking bird*.

When I suggested that he might spend 5 minutes of quiet meditation in his car before entering the "chaos" of his home, he responded between snorts of laughter that he didn't have time for *fucking meditation*, and yet despite his perceived indifference, he kept coming back until he didn't. One day his assistant called to notify us that Mark had *a mini-stroke.*

Mark had multiple risk factors for cerebrovascular disease including high blood pressure, high cholesterol, and excess weight. Still, at 52 years old, he was too young to have had a stroke. The morning of our scheduled appointment, Mark's assistant drove him to the emergency room because he was feeling off. Within minutes he was rushed into the operating room and injected with tPA (tissue plasminogen activator) to open up the blood clot that was obstructing blood flow to his brain. Because of the speed with which he arrived at the emergency room, Mark did not suffer permanent damage or die.

I saw Mark back in my office about 6 weeks after the incident. He was still somewhat shaken by the experience. He told me that as a result of what had happened, he was started on multiple new medications and was told that if he did not make major changes in his life that next time, *and there would be a next time*, he could die. So, in service of his brain, Mark began to slowly incorporate some of the changes that we had discussed. He limited his meals at restaurants. He started going to the gym during his lunch hour and meeting with a trainer on the weekends. As Mark began to make these changes, not only did he begin to lose weight but also his blood pressure dropped, his cholesterol levels improved, and he was even able to discontinue a few of his medications. But his stress, something equally important to his risk reduction, was not something he believed he could change. The work had to be done, he said, and his family life was just chaotic and out of his hands. He did not have the time, interest, or patience for meditation, breathing exercises, anger management, nature walks or any other *voo-doo* that I suggested might help. Instead, Mark was self-medicating with alcohol. Instead of addressing his hunger for ease, he was numbing. And that was not something he was willing to give up either.

Nonetheless, he was feeling better overall and was satisfied with the improvements in his health. After several months, his workload abruptly increased as a result of a widely publicized legal case. As his work intensified, so too did his stress level. His response was to drink even more except that it was no longer working. It seemed that the alcohol no longer took the edge off but was adding to the edge. He started to feel more anxious and irritable. His sleep began to suffer, and he became even more impatient with his wife and kids, resulting in more turmoil at home.

I was never a drinker. I made it through college barely noticing alcohol. In medical school I drank on rare occasions, like marking the end of final exams. And even as a resident, I had little interest outside of the occasional extracurricular activities. My life did not allow for the kind of socializing that resulted in the regular consumption of alcohol. Nor did my goody-two-shoes disposition. It was only when I started working that I realized that alcohol was always present, particularly in the workplace, and that it had become a more regular part of my life. Holding a glass of wine, and when I hung out with the men, a glass of scotch, became not only a social ritual but also a positioning. I could work like one of the guys, I could hang like one of the guys, and I could drink like one of the guys. That positioning, I felt, was important to my professional standing. It was, in fact, in the midst of my position as medical director that I realized my own desire to take the edge off. I had just created a niche program and was getting praise for my clinical work and for the educational and administrative programs I was involved in. With these accolades came responsibility but also anxiety and frustrations. I remember many nights when I would come home utterly exhausted. Sometimes, by the time I arrived, the rest of my family had already had dinner together, which only added to my angst. Family dinners had always been non-negotiable in our home. When my husband asked if I wanted dinner, there were times when I would just rather have wine. Like many adults, I began to enjoy wine not only at dinner parties and events but increasingly after a long day. I never thought twice about it. I kept to a glass per night. I never drank alone, and wine was so commonplace and well regarded that there was no reason to question its use.

My shift mirrored a cultural shift in regard to alcohol. We find alcohol at all our professional gatherings, at all our social gatherings, and at all our family gatherings. Work events, yoga classes, educational programs, dinner parties, and even kids' birthday parties and afternoon playdates all include alcohol, and casual drinking became a part of every culture and social space we inhabit. A recent survey of US adults showed that that nearly 73% drink alcohol. While as a society we focus on alcoholism, we ignore the casual drinking that has become commonplace and can transition to high-risk drinking or alcohol use disorder. In 2019 nearly 15 million people were classified as having alcohol use disorder which is characterized by an inability to stop or control alcohol use despite adverse social or health consequences, severe or mild. You don't need to have suffered a DUI or drink alone or drink for breakfast for alcohol to have an effect on your life.

Perhaps us doctors are partially to blame. For decades we have preached the benefits of wine and alcohol. We have touted the antioxidants, the benefits to cardiovascular health among other claims while ignoring the data that shows the adverse effects of even "casual" alcohol consumption. The presumed health benefits have lulled us into using alcohol more readily, more avidly, and without hesitation. But alcohol is a drug that has short- and long term effects on the brain and the body, influencing multiple aspects of mood, cognition, behavior, and health.

Alcohol's initial sedative effects come about through the release of gamma-aminobutyric acid (GABA), the same neurotransmitter responsible for the calming effect of benzodiazepines such as Valium or Ativan. Alcohol promotes the release of other sedating neurotransmitters such as glycine and adenosine, all of which result in an overall feeling of ease and relaxation in the body in the short term. These neurotransmitters are also responsible for the other sedating properties of alcohol, including slower reaction times, slower speech, reduced cognition, as well as memory deficits.

While alcohol is primarily known for its sedative effects, it has stimulatory effects as well. These include positive features such as greater energy, excitability, and even confidence. But alcohol also causes increased heart rate, anxiety, irritability, and aggressive behavior. In the end these unwanted effects contribute to the need to drink more in order to return to the experience of calm. Alcohol also triggers the release of dopamine, serotonin, and other endorphins. These neurotransmitters provide a feeling of pleasure and reward, but these are temporary and ultimately promote the habitual use of alcohol. This is also why a greater amount of alcohol is needed to recreate the feeling of calm. Finally, the long-term effect of alcohol is a reduced function of GABA and glutamate receptors, making the brain more excitable, and the person more anxious and irritable overall. This is precisely what Mark was experiencing.

The effect of alcohol on mood and wellbeing is compounded by its negative effects on sleep duration and sleep quality. Insomnia is the most common sleep disorder related to alcohol and is defined as difficulty with sleep initiation, duration, consolidation, or sleep quality. While alcohol induces sleepiness at first, it also causes sleep disruptions and awakenings. Regular drinkers might notice that while they fall asleep soon after drinking that they awaken in the middle of the night. Alcohol also disrupts sleep architecture, meaning that REM and non-REM sleep cycles are altered, preventing deep sleep, and diminishing the restorative quality of sleep. The overall effect is daytime fatigue and somnolence, further adding to irritability and anxiety.

The REM cycle is also when we consolidate memories and information. By affecting the quality and duration of REM sleep, alcohol impairs learning, memory, and cognition. Studies show that alcohol impairs learning and the acquisition of new information. This effect has been described as a failure to process information "deeply" as well as a "slowing of the processing rate" of information. So, while alcohol will momentarily "take the edge off," in the long run it contributes to greater mood disturbances, reduced productivity, and impaired memory and cognition. These unintended consequences are particularly impactful in high-functioning professionals like Mark who cannot afford the diminished capacity. So, while Mark was using alcohol to promote a greater sense of ease and wellbeing, he was in fact contributing to the opposite.

Lastly, while studies do show health benefits of alcohol, many demonstrate negative effects on health. Alcohol is touted for its cardioprotective benefits, but in excess alcohol can actually destroy the architecture of the heart through a stretching out of the heart muscle, which may ultimately progress to cardiomyopathy and heart failure. Regular drinking can also result in damage of the liver and pancreas and is associated with numerous cancers, including colon cancer, esophageal cancer, head and neck cancers, and breast cancer. In fact, as little as 10 grams of alcohol, which is found in one drink, when consumed daily, increases the risk of breast cancer risk by 15%. Not to mention the weight gain. Alcohol is not only a source of empty calories but also a cause of disinhibition which results in greater food and calorie intake, and it increases appetite by altering hunger hormones. Alcohol use interferes with leptin, which, as we have discussed, signals energy sufficiency to the brain.

It was not until the pandemic that I realized how I was using alcohol to counter my own anxiety, and it was contributing to poor sleep, irritability, reduced productivity, and more anxiety, not to mention weight gain. Change in routine, worry, and boredom had fueled a rise in alcohol consumption in Americans as a whole. In fact, a study published during the first 6 months of the pandemic revealed alcohol consumption increased by 14% as compared to the year prior, and 17% in women. Heavy drinking during this time escalated by 41% in woman. Given the pervasiveness of alcohol use, no one was questioning it, myself included at first. But as a physician, I knew that once you *think* that you might be drinking too much, then you are drinking too much, and there was no turning back.

In the midst of Mark's work overload, he had another scare. Months of sleeplessness and stress had resulted in a syncopal episode at the office, where he had collapsed and was found down by his assistant, landing him back in the hospital for several days of tests and observation. He had not had another stroke, but the warning was clear. The post-hospitalized Mark was a receptive Mark. This was an opportunity in which he was motivated to make change. In addition to the dietary and activity goals we had set, I challenged Mark to a 1-month experiment without alcohol. Much to my surprise, he was amenable. While he did not quit drinking altogether, his 1-month abstinence resulted in considerably less alcohol use overall as dry month challenges often do. This change also became a catalyst for other changes in his life. Mark made a concerted effort to reduce his load at work. He began to defer cases and pass them off to his partners. He began meditating, first in the car before coming home but then, noting the change in his demeanor, he made meditation a more structured part of his night-time routine. All of this had a positive effect on his relationship with his wife as well. He took a greater interest in taking time to be with her and the kids, and she took a greater interest in him. She began to cook and prepare healthy meals at home and hired a personal trainer to come to the house on weekends so that they could engage in activity together. Over time, Mark realized that his desire to numb was really a hunger for respite, a hunger for ease. Ease in his work life, ease in his relationship with his wife, ease in his relationship with his children, and ease in his relationship and expectations with himself. He acknowledged the need to rethink his obsession with work and to create deeper connection with his wife and children.

One day, about a year after his stroke, Mark came into the office for his follow-up. He referenced a legal case that had made headlines in the news.

"Hear about that, doc?" he asked.

I had.

"The case could've been mine, but I said no." He grinned.

It was a sign he had finally addressed the overworking that drove his hunger for ease, a hunger that he would no longer need to numb.

HUNGRY
TO BE VALUED

LEE WAS A YOUNG mother of two, a Harvard grad and an associ-
ate in a financial consulting firm. Lee told me that for the past
10 years she had worked 100 hours a week and had given up all
her lifelong habits—exercise, healthy eating, and tai chi, which
was her meditative practice since childhood. As a result, Lee had
gained over 100 pounds and was interested in a referral for bariatric surgery. She was just too overwhelmed by the weight gain
and the changes that she needed to make to do it any other way.
On the face of it, this was yet another story of work getting in the
way of wellbeing.

But Lee shared a deeper story. Lee told me that when she
was hired, she was the youngest in the firm and the only woman.
This had made her proud but also painstakingly dutiful. Lee described consistently taking on more than she should and always
helping before being asked, resulting not only in long hours but
also neglect of herself and her family. Over the previous 10 years,
she never took maternity leave, sick days, or family time. She was
so dedicated to her work that when her 7-year-old was getting
emergency surgery for appendicitis, she didn't take the day off,
but rather took her laptop into the hospital waiting room to work
while the surgeons operated on him down the hall. When she

finally told her senior partner why she was not in the office, he chastised her for not responding to a client in a timely manner.

"He did not even acknowledge that my child was having surgery and still I was working," she said.

Despite her diligence and loyalty, Lee had been passed up for a raise and also for a promotion to partner while a younger male colleague, who notably brought in fewer clients, was promoted in her stead. This only encouraged her to work more and harder, but it seemed that the more she did, the less she was seen or valued.

"It's like I am invisible!" she said, as if reading my mind.

I had experienced this anguish too. When I finally decided to quit my GI fellowship, I was offered a fellowship opportunity by my program director to explore my next steps. It had occurred to me that I wanted to focus on health, not disease, to focus on prevention, not disability, and so I explored functional medicine, alternative medicine, and holistic practices and ultimately landed on obesity and nutrition.

Back in 2005, we were in the midst of the obesity epidemic that had begun 20 years prior. The CDC had documented the steady and unrelenting rise of obesity in the United States, which had, by that time, reached a prevalence rate of 30% in certain states. (At the time of this writing, the prevalence of obesity in the US is greater than 40%.) But despite the pervasiveness, physicians were not educated on how to manage obesity and, as a result, were not educating our patients either, so I set out to educate myself. With the support of my program director, I used that year as a self-directed fellowship in clinical nutrition and obesity medicine. I read books and journals, visited various clinics, and attended conferences around the country. By the end of the year, I had an audacious plan. I would spearhead a comprehensive medical weight loss program at my very own institution.

It is hard to remember exactly what happened after I shared my plan with my chairman—everything happened so fast—but before I knew it, I was searching "How to Write a Business Plan" on the internet and was drafting my own. I knew that obesity affected every subspeciality in medicine, including patient outcomes, which of course helped my case for the program. I also knew that collaborating with my surgical colleagues would be of benefit as bariatric surgery had shed its murky reputation to become both well received by the public and lucrative for medical institutions. All of this went into the business plan. Several months later, one morning after a long night on call, I received a page to come to the executive offices of the hospital administration. On my way down, I stopped to drop some Visine in my eyes and Chapstick on my lips before I pulled open the heavy wooden doors. I was ushered into an office where several people were already seated, including senior administrators and the director of the bariatric surgery program. The hospital VP stood at a white board and scribbled a flow diagram for the new Center for Weight Loss. In one box, she wrote the name of the surgical director. In an adjacent box she wrote mine. And that is how I learned of my position as Medical Director of the Center for Weight Loss.

I was both elated and shocked. I had just wanted a job; *medical director* was not what I had expected. I felt gratitude and also indebted. An indebtedness that I now know colored my positioning and many of my actions. Later that week I was called in by a senior physician in my department.

"Adrienne, I have seen your contract, and you are being *grossly* underpaid." He encouraged me to negotiate my terms and my salary.

Grossly underpaid? Was he kidding? I would have worked for free I was so smitten.

Indebted.

To what degree I conspired in my own invisibility I can only imagine. I started my position several months later and hit the ground running. Given that this was a new program, my program, and there were no mentors, no prototypes, or anything else of the sort, I was given free rein to do what I wanted, and that was a privilege and a show of faith for which I am still grateful. I built the clinical structure of a medical weight loss program which grew exponentially that year and every year thereafter. I worked with my surgical colleagues to build a perioperative program for the bariatric surgery patients to optimize their health and nutritional status before and after surgery. I served on committees for the care of the obese patients in the medical center. I educated other doctors on the science and medicine of obesity, how obesity impacted their patients and their work, and how our weight loss program could help. I developed programs across multiple disciplines for weight loss, for example, before orthopedic surgery and hernia repair and other elective surgeries to improve postoperative outcomes. I participated in committees for transplant patients to help obese patients lose weight so they would qualify for new hearts and livers and lungs. Basically, every department in the hospital could benefit from our work.

I created an educational curriculum and elective for medical students, residents, and fellows who wanted to rotate with me and learn about obesity medicine. A few of those residents went on to specialize in obesity medicine themselves. I created an annual continuing medical education program for physicians and gave numerous lectures and grand rounds at my own and other institutions. I took the obesity medicine boards and then became a question writer for the boards myself. I participated in the publication of international guidelines for the care of bariatric surgery patients and gathered national experts to contribute to my own textbook, *A Clinician's Guide to the Treatment of Obesity Medicine*, that became recommended reading for other doctors who wished to specialize in this area. I basked in my success, and in the size-2 pencil skirts I would wear to work. And basked in the knowing that others saw and acknowledged my success. I recalled my days as a chubby girl with frizzy hair and fantasized about returning to Dallas to show them what *Arafat's granddaughter* was up to these days. Suffice it to say that my success felt like retribution.

It was only then, after 7 years of doing that work, after proving without a question of a doubt to be of value, that I took the advice of my attending from many years prior to ask for a salary that was in line with my efforts from the start, not to mention the 7 years during which I had never received a pay raise. I was nervous as I walked into the office, but my confidence grew as I recounted every financial spreadsheet, evaluation, letter of recommendation, lecture, publication, award, and accomplishment I had collected like treasures. By the time I was done, even I was surprised by all that I had accomplished in that relatively short period of time. It was one of the few times that I acknowledged my own value. But I was alone in that sentiment. It took only a minute before I was told *no*. Not only was the answer *no*, but I was criticized. I could have done more, others had, like the most prolific proceduralist in the institution, to whom I was compared to in making that point. Maybe in a few years I would deserve that raise, but not then. The truth is I didn't really care about the money. It wasn't about money; it was about value. And in that moment, I could not have felt more undervalued.

I sensed that Lee felt that way too. But Lee would not do anything about it, and neither did I, not then at least.

In his book, *Lost Connections*, Johann Hari describes the work of professor and epidemiologist Dr. Michael Marmot, who was commissioned by the British government to study health disparities in British civil servants. His work led to a large prospective study, named the Whitehall Study for the area in London in which they were conducted. Marmot was commissioned to determine the cause for a wave of suicide among tax collectors in the British government. He found that employees became distressed when their efforts were not recognized and identified this lack of recognition as the precipitant of severe depression. Tax inspectors who were diligent and produced good work but who went unnoticed for their efforts were more depressed than were those who did a poor job or mediocre job, so much so that it was resulting in suicide. Dr. Marmot's data showed that employees' mental health and wellbeing was contingent on recognition of efforts in the workplace. He described this as "a lack of balance between efforts and rewards," essentially a failure to be valued.

The imbalance between effort and reward is common in the workplace and particularly in large organizations in which individual efforts often go unnoticed. When you are not *seen* for your efforts, you are in a way rendered *invisible*. When you are not valued for your unique contributions, you invariably conclude that you as an individual are not valued. I wonder if this is deliberate as a means to engender greater effort or productivity by negating one's contribution and worth? That seems to have been the case with Lee. Or a means to incite fear by suggesting that one is dispensable? But this outdated and patriarchal leadership style in the long run does the opposite of engendering effort or productivity. Negating one's value stifles creativity, ingenuity and drive and, in the end, extinguishes the potential for both personal growth and growth for the organization at large. But the detriment to the organization was not my problem, nor was it Lee's. What matters is that diminishment of one's worth and value creates a hunger to be valued. A hunger which when left unfulfilled seeks to be filled in other ways. At the end of our long conversation, I imagined that Lee had an *aha* moment. I imagined that she was going to walk out of my office and into her boss's and demand what she deserved. But at the end of the visit, she reiterated her request for a bariatric surgery referral. I should not have been surprised. I know from experience that awareness does not immediately translate into action. Certainly, Lee qualified for bariatric surgery, and there was no reason that I would not oblige. Lee would have to come to realize her true hunger on her own time, as did I.

HUNGRY
FOR BOUNDARIES

I'M NOT SURE HOW to describe my first impression of Justine. Not quite disheveled but something like that. It's not that I am judging. We are told in medical school that noting a patient's appearance is an important part of the exam. It speaks to their self-care and to the possible diagnosis. Do they have poor dentition, for example? That might be a setup for a bloodstream infection. Do they have yellow-stained finger nails? This might indicate a smoking history. But Justine stood out differently. She wore elaborate jewelry, a large diamond ring on one hand and several gemstones on the other. Her teeth were perfect, and she smelled like shampoo, so it wasn't a lack of hygiene. But her hair was unkempt, long, and unbrushed. She wore a washed-out and discolored T-shirt that didn't match her expensive jewelry. She just seemed...uncared for. This is not typically what I notice when I examine my patients. My eyes are focused on the size of their thyroid, which might represent a goiter, or darkening of skin, which might signify insulin resistance. My ears are keen not to miss a murmur or any other irregular heart sounds. But Justine's appearance just struck me.

As if hearing my thoughts, Justine burst into tears. "Look at me, just look at me. I don't even have time to brush my hair!"

Justine told me that the reason for her weight gain was lack of time. She had never had a weight problem as a child. She does not crave sweets or snacks. But she just did not have the time to do the things she would do if she could. Justine said she had no time to prepare food, so she ate on the run. She had no time for exercise, so she didn't engage in any, nor did she have the time for adequate sleep. I imagined she had infants or toddlers at home but was surprised to hear her kids were older and in high school. They must have spent the bulk of their days at school; couldn't she find time for herself then?

But it was not just the kids. It was also her husband, who demanded warm home-cooked meals delivered to the office for lunch (not to mention home-cooked dinner when he gets home) and gets irritable when the house is not immaculate. *Can't she take time to prepare food for herself as she prepares food for him?* I wondered. *And why can't she get cleaning help at home?*

Justine was also responsible for her parents and her in-laws. She was the one who helped with doctors' visits as well as other mundane things like groceries and chores. I could understand that Justine had a full plate, but as she spoke, it occurred to me that what she perceived as a lack of time was really a lack of boundaries. She was fully accessible to her family, leaving little time or space for herself. Justine's true limitation was her inability to set boundaries with her family in a way that prioritized her own needs. And, ultimately, she did not value herself. Certainly, time is a precious resource, but time is also subjective, and time is something we create.

Scarcity of time has always been a personal challenge. Particularly when I was working at the hospital and had two small kids at home. Working at times 10 hours per day including some weekends with the hope of spending quality time with my kids left little time for much else. But in addition to that, I prioritized time for work or caretaking or chores or *something* over time for myself. True, the other activities were important, but fulfilling each and every demand at the exclusion of my own needs meant time would never come for me. And yet if there were ever an "emergency," someone needing my help, a work project, or even something trivial like arranging an extra playdate or making the homemade cookies instead of store bought for the kids' holiday parties, I would somehow find the time. When pressed for others, I always found time, but not for myself. It would be a long while before it finally occurred to me that time does not just exist, it is created. We don't *have* time; we create time for what is important and for what we value.

Despite Justine's constraints, she was really motivated. She asked if we could meet weekly, a great first step in creating time for herself. Justine considered prepping food for herself as she prepared food for her family. She started a walking program after dropping off her daughters at school. Not only was she losing weight but also, more importantly, she felt good. She felt more energetic, more vibrant. She even started to pull her hair back in a tight bun or a braid when she came to the office. But within a few months of getting started, Justine stopped making appointments and disappeared. When she returned 6 months later, she told me that her mother had knee replacement surgery, and she had to take over all of her mother's care, including bathing her, taking her to doctor's visits, grocery shopping, and cooking her meals. She was sorry for the lost time but was ready to resume.

Once again, we began to see each other weekly. And once again her body responded immediately. It was as if her body, too, was grateful for the time and care she showed it. She seemed to be thriving under those conditions. Her mood, her demeanor, everything about her reflected this change in her disposition, and I was reminded about the resilience of the human spirit and our fundamental desire to be well. It is not just about weight, but about wellbeing.

We worked together for several more months until once again she disappeared. I must admit that I was disappointed. It took Justine nearly a year to return. When she did, she told me that her husband had a health scare. While she nursed him back to health, and ironically helped him lose 15 pounds in the process, her own health had declined. He had gone back to work stronger than before, and she was left with her old habits. But once again, Justine was ready to resume. She really did seem to have the intention, but perhaps, once again, she just could not find the time. Justine lasted no more than 2 weeks before she disappeared for the last time.

Time does not exist, it is created.

Justine is not alone. Time is invariably perceived as a barrier for many if not most of my patients. Lack of time is the reason they cannot prepare wholesome food, engage in exercise, get adequate sleep, or make time for themselves in some other way, not recognizing that time is in their control. Appropriating time for their own care is a matter of priorities, values, and boundaries. The true limitation is their inability to prioritize themselves, to *make* time for themselves and their fundamental needs. This *is* a matter of setting boundaries. This lack of insight misdirects their focus on the scarcity of time, a belief that disempowers them and ultimately averts their attention from the true barrier.

When we consistently dismiss ourselves in the service of other people and other things, no matter how noble or important, we will never set the boundaries that makes us a priority. Someone or something will consistently take precedent over our own wellbeing. Making time for ourselves is a mindset. There will never be time if we do not create time, and Justine exemplifies this truth. Justine will find time when she sees herself worthy of time. Only when

Justine acknowledges her true hunger, her hunger for boundaries, will she find the time necessary for her care and her wellbeing.

HUNGRY
FOR ACCEPTANCE

I HAD TO CHECK the chart twice when I met Adele. I had expected a 56-year-old woman. Yes, the chart did say *56*, but Adele did *not* look as if she was in her 50s. My clientele, for lack of a better phrase, are well put together. I did work in the heart of Beverly Hills, and my patients were typically professional and affluent, perhaps in the industry or, if not, influenced by it. As a result, they wore beautiful clothes, had nice jewelry, and often, too, had aesthetic procedures that made them look youthful. But still Adele stood out.

She was not overdressed, casual in cargo pants and a top, her hair effortlessly pulled back from her face. Her skin glowed with barely a trace of makeup, but most notable to me was her physique. I could make out the outline of her shoulder muscle and biceps through her top. *This is certainly not a weight loss consult.*

As she sat, Adele immediately pulled out her phone and started to scroll through photos of herself over the last 5 years. She had made her career as a professional dancer since her early 20s and had danced alongside the greatest performers well into her 40s. She transitioned from dancing to a successful business creating high-performance dancewear. Despite the end of her formal dancing career, she still maintained a high-level physical fitness, training up to 2, sometimes 3, hours daily. Adele told me that she engaged in this level of activity not only for sport but also for her business. She was well-known in the industry, and her brand was dependent on her physique.

Adele was coming to see me because of weight gain that she had experienced over the previous few years. And she really was concerned with the change in her body composition. Not only had she noted "extra padding," she said as she grabbed her mid-section to illustrate, but also her body had gone soft. She no longer had the muscle definition that she was used to despite the fact that nothing in her diet or lifestyle had changed. I watched as she pulled at the miniscule amount of flesh at her mid-section, still not entirely clear on her source of discontent.

Adele pulled out a binder filled with papers. Over the previous year, she had seen a whole host of doctors, fitness instructors, and related professionals. She had blood tests, x-rays, and numerous other tests to determine a cause to these changes. After flipping through the litany of papers and reports, she concluded in tears that nothing was wrong with her.

"But something is wrong!" she pleaded.

As I scanned her binder, I noted that indeed she had many tests and that they were pristine with the exception for an age-appropriate change in her hormone levels that indicated she had undergone menopause as she was already aware. She had recently started and stopped hormone therapy due to lack of effect.

I asked Adele how much weight she had gained anyway. It turned out that she really hadn't. She had always been 125 pounds. And she weighed in on my scale, with clothes and all, pretty much the same. When she acknowledged this fact, she followed with how much she hated her body. It was so soft and *mushy*.

"Why" she asked me again, "is my body changing?"

I see many patients around menopause as it is a time in which the body transforms. *Nothing has changed*, is often what women tell me in terms of their diet and lifestyle. It may be true that their eating and activity has not changed, but certainly, something *has* changed.

The average age of menopause is 51, but most women will experience it sometime between the ages of 40 and 58. While menopause is officially defined as the absence of menses for a full year, the symptoms of menopause can precede this by up to 8 years and include mood disturbance, sleep disturbances, hot flashes, change in sexual drive, skin and hair changes, and changes in body composition, including a reduction in muscle mass, an increase in fat mass, weight gain, and a change in the distribution of fat to the abdomen.

I explained all of these changes to Adele and shared that while she had warded off those effects better than most, she likely would not be able to prevent them completely. With time, her body, *all bodies*, would change. As I spoke, I could see the tension building in her face. *This is not what she wishes to hear.* Maybe there is another test, another supplement, a medication that she had not tried.

While I am not the same age as Adele, I can understand her resistance at this change. I, too, get frustrated with the changes that I experience in my body. I am frustrated by my gray hair that now requires attention every 2 weeks. I am frustrated by the laxity of my skin despite my rigorous exercise routine. I am frustrated with dark spots that have popped up on my face. And I am frustrated by the recent sag I notice above my jawline. I am certain I am too young for that. But I am also keenly aware that I would kill for the things that frustrated me 10 years ago, and I am certain that 10 years from now, I will likely reminisce and yearn the present me. Change is inevitable, I cannot evade time, and those are things I must accept.

I smiled at Adele. I could appreciate that the changes are difficult for her to accept. Especially since she has maintained a youthful physique all of her life. I could also understand how difficult it must be for her to try to keep up in a world of younger celebrities who consistently remind her of her age and perhaps also of her mortality. I could help Adele tweak her diet, I could help her with a preventive lifestyle, I could help normalize her experience, but I could not change the reality—the reality that change is inevitable. Circumstances, people, bodies, and life change. Impermanence is the reality of our lives. Our relationships with our bodies give us an opportunity to grapple with the impermanence in our lives. To recognize that despite the wish otherwise, our lives will never stay the same, nor will they unravel exactly as we plan or as we wish. We can grieve. We can lament. But, ultimately, we must accept what is.

Acceptance was the antidote to Adele's suffering, but acceptance also allowed her to embrace her transformation. Therein lay an opportunity to be open and curious to her evolution and the beauty that awaited. Change does not need to be met with resignation, but we can find joy, gratitude, and opportunity in change by embracing our reality and accepting what is. Acceptance is what I believed Adele was hungry for, but not what she was willing to grant herself at that moment. She gathered the lab results and diagnostic test results that lay scattered my desk as she thanked me, somewhat insincerely, for my time. Perhaps the doctor she is scheduled to see later that week can help, she said as she left my office.

HUNGRY
FOR POWER

I MET BOB LESS than 2 weeks after his heart attack. He had been at a conference in Vail when he started feeling off. It began with some discomfort in his chest that he brushed off as indigestion. He also experienced some shortness of breath and overall weakness. He knew it was unusual, but he brushed that off too. Maybe altitude sickness, he thought. It was only when he returned home 2 days later that he decided to go to the doctor and was promptly sent to the emergency room, where he was diagnosed with a heart attack. The damage was so extensive that his heart function had dropped to an ejection fraction of 30%, and his kidneys had also been injured as a result of poor perfusion as well. After three stents, a defibrillator, and several days of observation in the hospital, he was sent home with a bagful of meds and a referral to see me for weight loss.

Incidentally, it is not just weight loss that will reduce risk factors and future cardiovascular event. Often, doctors and even patients fixate on weight loss when a weight-related health incident occurs. But the data is clear that certain lifestyle changes will reduce risk independent of weight loss. For example, a Mediterranean-style diet that prioritizes fruits and vegetables, grains and legumes, lean proteins, and mono and polyunsaturated fats and limits sweets, red meat, and sodium will reduce the risk of a second cardiovascular event, independent of weight loss. So will exercise, better sleep, and stress reduction, among other lifestyle changes.

Bob had a distinguished demeanor. I couldn't tell if it was his British accent or his impeccable clothing, but he had a certain authority.

"They told me I almost died, doctor," he said.

I had read his hospital record, and he was right; it is actually surprising that he was alive given the extensive damage to his heart. Sometimes, a life-altering event is the point at which change occurs. This is, perhaps, the silver lining. In the next hour we spent together, I got a full history from Bob. He had an extensive medical history that included hypertension, high cholesterol, pre-diabetes, sleep apnea, and gout. He was never married, which meant that he could put all his efforts into his work, and it had paid off, professionally at least. He was the founder of a well-known and successful international real estate investment firm. Following his lead, I reiterated that big changes were needed but worthwhile given the health benefits he would achieve. He agreed. But despite his eagerness, every suggestion was met with resistance.

"Let's talk about some strategies for eating out less."

"I'm sorry, doctor, but I do have to eat out. That's where I conduct my business and all the work happens."

We had a lot more to discuss, and I didn't want to push too soon, so I shifted gears.

"Ok, let's talk about sleep. Can we shoot for 8 hours—can we start with 7?"

"I am working on a big deal; I might even retire after this!" he said. "But I am working with China, and unfortunately, my sleep depends on their time zone until we get this done."

"How about activity? Can we get more activity into your day?"

"It's going to be tough to find time right now. I'm traveling 20 out of the next 30 days for work.

"I really want to do this, doctor," he said. "I really do, but with this deal in the works, some things are just impossible right now."

I didn't get the feeling that he was being dismissive. He sounded desiring, even apologetic for being non-committal, but despite his health scare, he genuinely felt he *could not* make any changes that might compromise his work. Bob had built an empire, was wildly successful and wealthy, but for all his authority, it struck me that he had no power. He was the boss and, yet, he was powerless.

"Fuck work," I wanted to say. Hadn't we agreed that he almost died? Who was in charge here anyway?

Despite my objectivity, sometimes I get triggered by my patients. Triggered by the desire to help, triggered by their seeming lack of willingness to help themselves. Triggered by their sense of powerlessness in the face of catastrophic need for change. Perhaps I am triggered because of my own history. My own self-proclaimed powerlessness. When I knew in my gut that I needed to pivot yet continued in an unworkable circumstance under the guise of powerlessness.

I was seemingly in a position of great authority when I felt my lack of power most acutely. I had spent nearly a decade in an academic institution. I had created my own sphere of expertise and was teaching, writing, and lecturing. My referrals came from department chairs and administrative VPs and other grateful and famous patients who spoke highly of me. I had a fancy title and a fancy coat. What else could I want? I had achieved more than I ever wanted, more than I could have ever imagined, and yet it was clear that I wanted more, much more. And I couldn't do it by staying. I needed space, independence, autonomy, more sleep, time, nature, creativity, and possibility. But first I needed to claim my power, without which none of that would be possible.

It started as a suspicion, this knowing that I needed to leave, a nagging inside of me. I tried to ignore it. But as time went on, it persisted and became more annoying, vexing, and tormenting until the nag was raging inside of me. Despite my position of authority, I felt powerless. I had no authority over my own life. My fear was so strong that I tried everything in my power to dismiss my intuition. Self-doubt, self-deprecation, and false narratives to will my inner voice to back off.

You cannot do it!

You are too inexperienced, too small, too scared…too inadequate.

We fear change because of the uncertainty. Particularly when we are enjoying a position of authority and security and even more so when our position appears glamorous to those on the outside. *Why would you do such a thing?* I envisioned people saying, or, rather, I imagined they would just whisper my idiocy behind my back. We are so fearful that we chose to comply with the status quo, even when the status quo is killing us. And that fear robs us of our power.

Take back your power! I wanted to yell at Bob. *This was a warning that your present template is no longer working!*

At the end of our visit, Bob thanked me. He told me he was committed but as he mentioned already, he was months away from a big acquisition and could not set aside the time for anything else. As he left, Bob said, "I'll be back. I *will* be back!"

I smiled as I led him out of my office.

A few months later, Bob's referring doctor called me. He had unfortunate news to share. Bob had suffered a massive heart attack and died.

Hungry
for Autonomy

Amelia was a partner at a global tech company that serviced partners around the world. Her work was arduous, requiring long hours and frequent travel overseas, which took her away from home weeks at a time. Having recently completed a big project, she was in Los Angeles for an extended period and wanted to take the opportunity to focus on some personal projects including tackling her weight. A decade of long work hours and frequent travel had resulted in significant weight gain, and she was motivated to address it. Amelia began a daily walking regimen and changed her diet, and she started to lose weight consistently for the first 6 months of our time together. Her mood was uplifted, and she said she had more energy than she had in years. Then she was thrown into a big project at work. Her work frequently pulled her into one thing or another quite abruptly. Soon, her visits with me started to become less frequent. Visits every 2 weeks turned into every 4, then even less frequently than that. Soon, she stopped coming in altogether. Amelia returned to see me nearly a year later. During that time she had regained over 40 pounds.

Around the same time, Amelia began to experience vertigo—a disturbing dizziness in which she experienced her surroundings as spinning around her. An extensive medical workup that took her to the best medical centers across the country failed to reveal an organic cause to the vertigo that was interfering with her work and her quality of life. Meanwhile, our prior strategies including dietary plans and medications were no longer effective. She felt hungry all the time and was eating and snacking excessively. Amelia returned frustrated and angry and for the first time seemed to resent her work.

When we first met, she had spoken of her job with such pride. She basked in her recent partnership at the firm, in the caliber of her clients, in the interesting things they were doing. And she basked in the reputation she had secured among her colleagues, the reputation that made her frequently called upon as had been the case before she stopped seeing me the year before.

But now she was resentful. While she had loved her work, she was tired of the long hours, tired of the frequent travel, tired of her inability to spend time with her boys, tired of the absence of personal time (not to mention how it interfered with her health goals). Amelia was also increasingly resentful of the fact that her time was never her own. She lamented that even her long-planned summer vacation had been cancelled by a last-minute hand-off by her senior partners.

I suggested that her weight regain and perhaps even the annoying room spinning that was not traceable to any organic etiology might be a sign that she needed to reexamine her current path. Maybe it indicated that something in her life needed to change. I wondered if a hunger for autonomy was driving her compulsion to eat as well as her annoying vertigo. You can love your work and still resent the absence of autonomy. This I knew.

Not everyone is like you, I admonished myself, knowing my personal bias.

It had been nearly a decade since that day that I had been named medical director of the center for weight loss. I had thrived in the position and had made a reputation for myself as a leader. And yet I did not feel like one. While I was respected, I was not valued. While I had the authority to create the program, I did not have autonomy and was increasingly stymied from professional growth. Though I became more senior, my time was becoming increasingly micro-managed. RVUs, time and effort, and all the other metrics put into place by the institution to ensure productivity were stifling my productivity, my creativity, and my desire to contribute. And finally, while I was regarded as a future member of the institution, it was becoming very clear to me that this was not my future.

I had been selected with a group of peers to join a year-long leadership program. In this program, budding physicians, executives, and administrators would be groomed to chart the path of the future of the institution. I remember a poignant moment when our group leader led us in an exercise to envision the future, to imagine how we saw ourselves in that future. And it was in that moment, sitting in that boardroom with my eyes closed, that it dawned on me.

This is not my future.

My hunger for perfection, my hunger for belonging, my hunger to please, my hunger for approval, and my hunger to be valued had brought me to that point. It had given me much success, much learning, much growth, and much heartache, and there was where it would end. It was one thing to disregard myself all those years, studying by the light of the fridge in silence, acquiescing to untimely moves and untimely transitions without protest, deferring to others, chastising myself, restricting myself, doing too much, trying too hard, trying to prove, and wanting to please. I had earned my right for autonomy, and now I was finally going to seize it. I left the leadership meeting early that day and went back to my office, where I drafted my letter of resignation.

According to self-determination theory, a theory of human motivation, personality, and development, autonomy is a basic psychological need necessary for growth and wellbeing. When people feel autonomous, they believe their needs, motivations, desires, and actions to be aligned. Autonomy encapsulates a feeling of choice and living in congruence with one's personal values and convictions. Additionally, validated psychological scales have shown autonomy to be a key domain of psychological wellbeing whereas lack of autonomy has been associated with feeling alienated, helpless, and even hostile and destructive.

Lack of autonomy has been shown to be a significant contributor to physician dissatisfaction and burnout. Physician burnout, characterized by emotional exhaustion, depersonalization, and a feeling of low personal accomplishment, results not only in poor emotional wellbeing for physicians but also in suboptimal patient care. Studies have consistently shown lack of autonomy as a central factor to burnout, but this phenomenon, of course, is not limited to physicians.

Like me, Amelia knew that something had to change. She was poised for change and yet immobilized. Month after month she would return more frustrated, more despondent. All the while struggling with her weight and the vertigo. Finally, the vertigo became so severe that she had to take sick leave. She decided to take a leave not only from work but from everything and left for her parents' cabin in Montana, alone. With her newfound time, she began to do things she hadn't done in years, like gardening and painting. She also started cooking wholesome meals, taking long walks, and spending time in meditation and solitude. After a month of this new routine, Amelia woke up one day to find the vertigo, abruptly, was gone. Just like that. After over a year of anguish, it was gone and never returned. Was it a coincidence or was her vertigo (and weight gain) an indication of Amelia's hunger for autonomy?

It is not a stretch to think the two were related. Dr. Marmot's extensive research of the British Civil Service demonstrated the correlation between autonomy and illness. In the Whitehall studies, Marmot sought to determine social determinants of health. His findings showed that there was an association between employee rank and mortality such that those individuals in the lower ranks, such as messengers and doorkeepers, had *3 times* higher mortality than the highest-ranked employees. Initially, this disparity seemed to be associated with a prevalence of risk factors in the lower ranks. For example, lower-ranked individuals had a higher prevalence of obesity and smoking and higher blood pressure. However, even after controlling for these variables, the lower-ranked employees still suffered twice the cardiovascular mortality than those in the highest ranks.

In a second set of studies, named Whitehall II, the susceptibility to cardiovascular disease and cardiac mortality specifically was correlated with employee rank in both men and women. Marmot also found correlations in other disease states, including certain cancers, chronic lung disease, and gastrointestinal disease. In what has subsequently been termed *Status Syndrome*, it is argued that socio-economic status is an important determinant of health outcomes even after controlling for the effects of income, education, and risk factors on health. Marmot described this as the benefit of "being in control" of one's life, in essence *autonomy*, and the lack of autonomy as detrimental to one's health.

Autonomy is a fundamental psychological need and an important determinant of psychological and physiologic wellbeing. Given this, it is not far-fetched to consider that Amelia's hunger for autonomy manifested as vertigo, weight gain, and overall disease. Certainly, work is necessary and the love of work desired, yet when it encroaches on our fundamental need for autonomy, we suffer a hunger that costs us not only our emotional wellbeing but also our physical wellbeing.

Hungry
for Creativity

C<small>AROL</small> <small>HAD RECENTLY RETIRED</small> from her position at the Department of Justice. As a career judge, she was very much married to her work and was not quite mentally ready for retirement, but she was eligible and because her husband, who was diagnosed with Parkinson's disease several years before, was declining in health, she decided it was finally time to step away. Since her retirement, her own health had also suffered somewhat. She had developed hypertension and insulin resistance, which her family doctor had attributed to weight gain. In discussing the timing of her weight gain, Carol described a kind of restlessness. She did miss her work, the intellectual stimulation, and her interaction with like-minded peers, but she did not feel the restlessness was totally a result of her retirement. She had adjusted to the change of pace, and, while nostalgic, she was not desirous to return. She also did not feel her restlessness represented boredom. Between her husband, her grandkids, and her continued philanthropic work, she was busy enough. When I asked her about hobbies or what she did in her downtime, Carol laughed.

"You don't become a judge by knitting and gardening all day."

But it occurred to me that knitting, and gardening were exactly what Carol needed. What we could agree on by the end of the conversation was that the restlessness was distressing and was fueling her eating habits as well.

Carol's disposition reminded me of my own. I was always heavily invested in professional growth but never gave much thought to personal growth, and, in particular, I didn't give myself time for creativity or downtime, which was just wasteful in my view. But in fact, the data shows otherwise as did my personal experience. I was at the peak of my professional life when I started to experience the sort of restlessness that Carol describes. It was not the same as other restless moments I had experienced. I was not restless because of work. I had happily started my private practice soon after my resignation and was enjoying my professional autonomy. I did not feel restless due to my relationships or family life; while I had experienced much angst in balancing motherhood early in my career, in this moment I felt assured and at peace. My three children were thriving, and while my motherly duties were significant with a high-schooler, a middle-schooler, and a kindergartener, I was liberated from diapers and daycare and the other struggles of having small children. And one could say I was taking fairly good care of myself. I was getting more sleep than I had in decades, was cooking more than I ever had, and continued to make regular exercise a non-negotiable part of my life. So, what was so damned disconcerting?

While I did enjoy freedom in the many ways I described, I did not have freedom from the belief that my time should be spent exclusively in productive pursuits, so I spent every moment in that way. And with my many roles, personally and professionally, I was very particular about how I spent my time and guarded zealously against *waste*. Downtime, hobbies, and creativity were most certainly wasteful in my world view. I had always fantasized about playing drums, but I did not have time for that. I would never have considered art, and anyway, did not have the skill for that.

But cooking, that was a creative pursuit that was not so wasteful. Cooking for my family and kids was a priority. In a way, cooking was part of my work as I talked to patients about food all the time. For these reasons, I gave myself permission to enroll in a cooking class. For 10 weeks I spent 4 hours every Tuesday morning at The Gourmandise School, a local cooking school. In that course I learned knife skills; the basics of blanching, roasting, and searing; how to take apart a whole chicken and debone a fish. I learned to make gnocchi from scratch as well as eggs Benedict. But mostly I learned that "wasteful" creative pursuits were not wasteful at all; in fact, they were essential to wellbeing *and* productivity. I found myself experiencing an unexpected amount of joy during the class as well as tremendous peace of mind. This sense of ease trickled into the rest of my day and my week as did my sense of creativity. I became flooded with ideas, so much so that I bought a notebook to capture them all. Activities for me and the kids, projects around the house, ideas for writings and blog posts for my patients and online magazines. During this time I formulated my line of nutrition bars and supplements I called Dehl Nutrition. Engaging in creativity also made me open to taking on other creative endeavors, including starting to write this book.

My personal experience of the relationship between creative pursuits and my overall wellbeing are supported in numerous scientific studies. Creativity has been associated with greater happiness, reduced stress, improvements in anxiety and depression, and emotional regulation. In fact, in one study, creative activities such as journaling enhanced the ability to cope, increased the joy of discovery, and provided individuals the opportunity to reflect on their lives and derive significance from past events. Engaging in creative activity has also been shown to improve productivity, creative thinking, and problem solving. Studies have demonstrated the relationship between creativity and physical wellbeing. It has been shown that creative work evokes the para-sympathetic nervous system, reducing heart rate, blood pressure, and respiratory rate or the rate at which we breathe, opposing the sympathetic stress response. Creative activities also stimulate the release of endorphins from specific areas of the brain, affecting not only mood but also the brain cells themselves. Creative activity strengthens brain growth and brain activity by promoting greater connections between brain cells or neurons through the growth of dendrites—tiny projections of the neuron that receive and transmit information to other neurons. Creative activities also enhance communication between neurons through the production of acetylcholine, a neurotransmitter involved in memory and intellectual processes. Creative work has been shown to reduce dementia. In one study, individuals who colored regularly had reduced incidence of cognitive decline. Finally, engaging in creative activities has been shown to improve immune function. Taken together, these studies support the beneficial effects of creativity, particularly for older adults like Carol.

At a subsequent visit, I urged her to reconsider. I felt strongly that what Carol really needed was to engage in creative pursuit. Cooking, writing, crafting, music, planting. It would allow her to focus her attention on something more introspective, and perhaps by shifting from a task-oriented approach to an intuitive one, she would quiet the restlessness inside. The restlessness that compelled her to eat.

Carol was unsure but after some prodding, she disclosed that she used to paint as a young adult. In fact, she had considered art as her major in college but was encouraged by her parents to get a more practical degree and had settled on political science instead. Carol agreed to consider painting again. As the months progressed, she found that painting allowed her to process the transition in her life from career professional to retirement, to process her husband's progressive illness, and to begin to alleviate her restlessness overall. She became more mindful of her habitual snacking, which was responsible for the weight gain she had experienced. Carol also experienced improvements in her overall health. In addition to the 15 pounds that she lost, her blood sugar normalized and so did her blood pressure. Whether this was related to the weight loss or to the painting itself, I'm not sure, but the data supports both possibilities. More importantly she had satisfied her true hunger, her hunger for creativity.

Hungry
for Imagination

"Do you think I will ever change?" Blair asked, her eyes filling with tears. Blair was 23 years old, but in that moment, she looked like the little 8-year-old girl she had just described.

That was the first summer when Blair attended "fat camp," at the age of 8. This was followed by nutritionists, stimulants prescribed by her mother's doctor at age 13, and bariatric surgery at the age of 19. By the time she was 24, she had already experienced a lifetime of weight loss interventions. Each time she had managed to lose anywhere from 20 to, in the case of bariatric surgery, 100 pounds, only to suffer weight regain in the end. Blair also shared a long family history of obesity that she believed destined her to a lifetime of "fatness."

"My mom has been big all my life. So has my dad and my sister. Even my aunts and my grandmother are fat. Everyone is fat!' She sounded exasperated. "And I will be fat too," she said, looking down at herself, "no matter what I do."

It is easy to understand why Blair would think that she could never change, particularly since obesity has been so prevalent in her own life and the life of her family. It is difficult to imagine change when something is so ingrained in your history, but imagination is exactly what is needed.

"Change is something you need to believe in," I said. She looked at me with eyes both hopeful and suspicious. I imagined what she might be thinking. *She doesn't understand.* That's what most of my clients think.

Not too long before my first session with Blair, I had been asked to speak at a national bariatric surgery support group. Many in this group had been struggling with obesity since childhood and either had or were considering having bariatric surgery, meaning most had likely already exhausted diets and pills and other treatments for obesity. They were a highly knowledgeable and expectant group. And I was intimidated, worried that they had heard it all. What more could I possibly offer them? Just before I was to speak, I made my way to the restroom, passing a few ladies on my way in. As I went into the stall, I couldn't help but overhear their whispered conversation.

"That's the speaker," one of them said.

"*Her?*"

What was it in her voice? I wondered. Was it sarcasm or disdain?

"Just another *Barbie* who thinks she gets it," the other chimed in.

Barbie! I didn't know whether to object or to laugh.

What I would have paid to have had a Barbie that looked like me! my inner child thought. But Barbies with wide hips and thick eyebrows did not exist back then. I guessed that by looking at me now, they would never have suspected that I struggled. That I had spent my entire childhood, teenage years, and young adulthood obsessed with my body, putting myself on ridiculous diets and brooding over the numbers on the scale. While I hoped and prayed that I could identify myself differently, I could not have imagined doing so then either. My genetics were not defined by obesity in the same way as Blair's family, but we were not exactly the long and slender type. What these ladies at the support group and Blair sitting across from me did not know is that all that separates me now from that girl 30 years ago was the imagination that things could be different.

It is true that the genetics of obesity is well-documented. The best proof is in twin studies which show that monozygotic or identical twins who are raised apart have similar weights despite different upbringings. Studies of adopted children follow the same pattern. The weight of adoptees are more congruent with the weight of their biological parents as compared to their adoptive parents. In one Swedish study of 25,000 twin pairs, BMI or body mass index more closely resembled the biologic parent 70% of the time as compared to the adoptive parents. These and other studies show that there is a strong genetic component of body weight.

However, despite these associations and extensive mapping of the human genome, the search for genes that predict common obesity have been largely unsuccessful. Meaning we have not identified genes that code for garden-variety obesity. The genes identified to date are primarily for rare and uncommon genetic conditions, which do not relate to the average person. More importantly, the argument minimizing the role of genetics is far more persuasive than the argument for the genetics of obesity.

The rapid rise of obesity in the last 30 years speaks strongly against a genetic component in the etiology of this dramatic rise. Genetics cannot account for such rapid changes in a phenotype or a physical characteristic because genetic changes are very gradual and take time. As a result, environment is believed to be more significant than genetics in this regard. A perfect example of the influence of environment over genetics is in the Pima Indians, a tribe of Native Americans who migrated simultaneously to Southern Arizona and to Northern Sonora, Mexico. The migration of this genetically "same" tribe to two vastly different environments allows for us to evaluate the interplay between environment, genetics, and health outcomes such as obesity. On average, Pima Indians living in the United States are over 50 pounds heavier than Pima Indians who live in Mexico. Pima Indians residing in the US also have a much higher incidence of diabetes. This dramatic difference in weight and metabolic disease between these two genetically homogenous populations speaks to the strong environmental role to obesity that overrides any genetic predisposition.

This important impact of environment over genetics may also speak to epigenetics. As we have discussed, epigenetics is the way in which environmental factors modify the expression of our genes. We know that what we eat, how much we eat, exercise and sleep, and the traumas we have been exposed to—verbal, emotional, physical or otherwise—all impact our genes in an epigenetic manner, shaping our DNA and what is passed down to generations to come. Epigenetics, therefore, presents one mechanism by which not only our environment but also, more importantly, our choices shape our DNA to impact our health and wellbeing and the health and wellbeing of generations to come.

This knowing can be overwhelming but also awe-inspiring and empowering. This knowing is also a powerful endorsement for mindset. Mindset is the way in which we perceive ourselves, our attributes, our capabilities, and our possibilities. In essence, our mindset is the way in which we hold ourselves in mind. Decades of research in *implicit theory* have shown that people hold a range of beliefs regarding their personal abilities and attributes and that these beliefs directly impact their opportunities and possibilities. This theory describes two opposing mindsets, a fixed mindset and a growth mindset. A fixed mindset is a belief that our attributes are preset and, therefore, fixed and unchangeable. Imagine, for example, the child who has always been told she is smart. This child may imagine that she was born with her smartness; it is an endowed attribute and therefore fixed. This child might feel innately smart, but because of that she might also feel that it cannot be changed or improved upon and ends up getting stuck. By comparison, a child with a growth mindset may not feel that he or she has been born with an innate gift but is open to the possibility for growth and improvement. This child is more likely to take risks, to explore, and therefore create the conditions for growth. This mindset believes in potential, and this mindset requires *imagination.*

Researcher Dr. Carol Dweck, who developed the implicit theory, has shown that our mindset, which is often subconscious, can affect our motivation and our ability to succeed. Individuals who have a fixed mindset avoid challenges because of a fear of failure whereas those with a growth mindset view failure as an opportunity for growth and are more likely to engage in the activities in which growth and improvement are possible. This phenomenon has been demonstrated to hold true in every facet of life, education, athletics, business, and even health and weight.

In one study, overweight and obese individuals were categorized by their mindset concerning their weight. Those with a growth mindset who more strongly agreed with statements such as, *Weight is something you can change,* or *I usually feel confident in my ability to manage my weight* were less likely to gain weight following perceived dietary setbacks as compared to those who did not agree with such statements or beliefs. Individuals who have a growth mindset around weight were more likely to opt for healthier food choices as compared with those who did not. Individuals with a growth mindset were also more likely to achieve exercise goals and recommendations as compared to those who do not. Given their perspective, growth-minded individuals are more likely to adopt the behaviors that make weight loss possible. Finally, studies have shown that mindset can impact physiologic parameters as well. In a related study, researchers sought to determine the relationship between mindset and health metrics. Hotel attendants who had labor-intensive jobs were divided into two groups. Half the attendants were educated on the fact that their regular work activities were a form of physical activity whereas the other half were not given this counseling. After 4 weeks, the group that believed themselves to be physically active demonstrated greater reductions in blood pressure, waist-to-hip ratio (a surrogate for visceral or belly fat), body mass index, and body fat as compared with the control group who did not adopt this mindset nor the perception in higher degrees of physical activity. It is important to note that the change in these physiologic parameters was not attributable to a change in their activity because the degree of activity remained the same in these subjects. Rather, the change in physiologic parameters was dependent to the subjects' *perception* of their activity such that those individuals who now perceived themselves as getting more activity actually achieved a greater physiologic benefit.

These studies demonstrate the importance of mindset. In fact, the ability to successfully self-regulate in our present environment is dependent on mindset. A mindset, or the imagination that we can transcend both our genetics and our increasingly obesogenic environment. A fixed mindset invalidates our capacity for change and renders us powerless against the challenging environment that we live in. As the example of the Pima Indians demonstrates, the environment can override our genetics, but as the implicit theory teaches us, our mindset can override both. Certainly, Blair has genetic predisposition, but as the studies suggest, mindset, irrespective of genetics, can dictate her health behaviors and her health outcomes.

Blair was hungry for the possibility of something different. She was hungry for imagination. We began a relationship that continued for nearly a decade. She inherently possesses the capability to grow, to evolve, and to overcome both her environment and genetic predisposition; she just needed imagination that it was possible. Our work together allowed her to cultivate this knowing for herself. With time she fostered this innate wisdom and was able to call on it without my prompting or reminding. Blair lost nearly 175 pounds during our prolonged time together. She warded off the metabolic disease she believed she was destined for, and, most importantly, she dared to imagine and in doing so, dared to succeed.

Hungry
for Presence

It was clear from Scarlett's smooth face that she was young, but her eyes were aged and worn. When she shared her story, it was clear why. Scarlett had married early and become a mother by the age of 20 and had a second child the following year. But it was not the onus of marriage or the children that had frayed her, but the illness of her son. Soon after his second birthday, it was clear that Scarlett's son was not hitting his developmental milestones. His walking was delayed. His fine motor skills were delayed. And when his gait became grossly abnormal, they were advised to meet with a specialist. A series of tests and procedures revealed devastating news: Ariel had a rare form of muscular dystrophy. Genetic tests demonstrated this to be a novel disease that was poorly understood. All Scarlett knew was that her son would slowly deteriorate. He would lose his strength and his function and ultimately become wheelchair bound. Most devastating of all, Ariel would not survive past his teens. Scarlett shared that her son had already surpassed their expectations. The physical therapy, occupational therapy, and all the other resources that Scarlett had secured were slowing the progression of his disease. Despite the diagnosis and the threat of the impending outcome, he was thriving.

Meanwhile, Scarlett was not. Her son's illness was not only emotionally taxing but also incredibly time and resource intensive. Her entire existence was taking him to doctors and therapists, appointments, and treatments. When she was not shuffling him from one place to another, she was managing his medications, cooking meals that followed the highly specialized diet recommendations, and researching alternative therapies and ways to pay for the costly and experimental treatments. Scarlett did not interact with friends, she never had her hair or nails done, and she no longer practiced yoga or did anything that she had enjoyed prior to Ariel's illness. In addition, she had steadily gained weight. Scarlett did not care much about the weight gain, although it amounted to over 50 pounds in 6 years, but realized that her approach was not sustainable. She was depressed, anxious, disconnected from her friends and family, and, finally, her husband had insisted that she get help. After starting antidepressants and weekly visits with a therapist, she decided to tackle her lifestyle but was ambivalent. How could she care about her weight when her son was dying? How could she exercise when he could not walk on his own? Most distressing to her was the anticipation. How long he would live, how he would live, and when he would die. As a mother, I was heartbroken. What could I say? How could I comfort her? There was no comfort in words.

I wondered, was it possible in light of this terrifying outcome to just be present?

I would say that I myself have been a worrier all my life. So much so that when I was a child and a member of the monthly Sweet Pickle book series, the book that most resonated with me was *The Very Worried Walrus.* This was the story of a walrus who longed to ride a bicycle but was debilitated by his fear of all that could go wrong. In the story, the worried walrus conjured up all the possible misfortunes that might occur should he actually ride the bike. He imagined that he would fall in the middle of the street. The traffic would be so dense that the ambulance would be unable to reach him, so a helicopter would have to be called for him instead. Except that somehow, the helicopter would falter as well and ultimately, he would have to be rescued from the helicopter by rope. I still have a copy of that book at my bedside. As an adult it is funny to reflect on this memory and yet a reminder of the downside of our mind's practice of over-anticipating potential catastrophe as a means to cope with uncertainty.

Over the years, I have learned to manage my worry. I have learned tools that help me—positive self-talk, exercise, journaling—but nothing is more valuable than presence. I have yet to master the art of presence, but I know it to be essential to managing worry and to peace of mind in general. I experience moments of presence, like snuggling in bed with my daughter, embracing her as she watches cartoons. But, invariably, I become distracted by a thought of what I need to get done, and my mind wanders off into the future. Or moments when I get lost in the smell of eucalyptus on a morning run, only to be interrupted by a reminder of something unpleasant said by an acquaintance that takes me off ruminating about the past. And times when I am enjoying dinner with my family when a text message draws me to my phone and to an endless litany of emails and messages that await me. No, presence was not something I excelled at.

Not that I didn't try. I had taken meditation classes, read books, and even attended medical conferences on the topic. At one of these conferences, I was introduced to the Relaxation Response, a term coined by Dr. Herbert Benson, professor and cardiologist, that describes our ability to turn off the sympathetic response to stress and induce deep relaxation. As he describes in his book by the same name, there are many ways to elicit the Relaxation Response, including visualization, muscle relaxation, energy healing, acupuncture, massage, breathing techniques, prayer, meditation, tai chi, qi gong, and yoga. Relaxation can also be achieved by choosing a word, phrase, or prayer as a mantra to help drop one into a more relaxed state. Dr. Benson's research showed that by doing so, one could achieve immediate physiologic benefits such as reduced heart rate, blood pressure, and respiratory rate and an overall switch from a heightened sympathetic response to a relaxed parasympathetic response.

"Just this," the speaker had said. "When you are in the midst of ruminations and worry about the past or the future, cultivate presence by reminding yourself that all you need in this moment, all you have in this moment is *just this.*"

I closed my eyes. *Just this.* Wow, I remember thinking, intrigued by how much it resonated.

But still, it was a practice and a struggle. And then I received the lesson that no meditation class, book, or conference could teach me. It had been a busy year for me. I had made major changes to my medical practice; had launched Dehl Nutrition, the product line that I had dreamed up for years; started a podcast; *started this book*; and was active in several academic projects. Everything was great except that I was utterly overwhelmed. I found my mind constantly bouncing from one task to another, from writing my book to writing a lecture, from my kids to the dog, from what should I cook for dinner to when will I finish my charts or answer this email or pay that bill. I lacked focus, and I more poignantly lacked presence.

It was in the midst of this that I had made an appointment for my father to meet with his neurologist. He had first complained about his memory many years prior. I had just had my second child when he called me at the office. It was unusual to receive a call from him mid-day, so I excused myself from my patient to take the call. He relayed his concerns and asked if I could find a neuropsychiatrist, someone who could do cognitive testing and check his memory.

"Cognitive testing?" I laughed. "Because you forgot your keys?"

It had already been 6 months since my second child was born, and I felt I was still recovering from pregnancy brain. Forgetting my phone, forgetting my lunch, forgetting the names of the patients I had seen just that morning. I had even left my newborn in his stroller at my daughter's preschool that week. Only when I arrived at the car did I realize I had left my child.

"Come on, Dad!" I said, amused, and did not give it any more thought. He dropped it as well. Many years passed before he brought it up again. I was not convinced, but I arranged for cognitive testing anyway. The diagnosis came back as Mild Cognitive Decline. "It could just be normal aging; it could be something else," is what the doctor told us. At the time he was already in his mid-70s. Wasn't he allowed some mild cognitive decline? Sure, sometimes he repeated himself, but honestly, who didn't? I brushed off his and my mother's concerns once again, and a few more years passed.

But by then, things did seem different, and I could no longer deny that I was noticing something too. After much deliberation, we decided to repeat the neurocognitive and neuroimaging tests once more to determine what might have progressed in the interim. Was this really age-related cognitive decline, or was it something else? I must admit that I was bit worried. I went to my parents' home to join the telemedicine visit with the neurologist.

"Dr. Youdim," she said, looking at my father through the computer screen, "after reviewing the results, I can say with some certainty that you have Alzheimer's disease."

The words hit me like a slap in my face. I was still reeling when she pulled up the MRI images of his brain on our shared screen. My mind raced as she circled the white and black image of his temporal and parietal lobes with her little white cursor, indicating evidence for his disease. I dared not look at him yet but could see him sitting next to me, frozen, out of the corner of my eye.

What is going to happen to him?

We logged off the computer. I held his trembling hands in mine as the heat rose to my face.

Just this, I said to myself with a deep breath, *just this.* My mind continued to race.

Will he become totally dependent on my mother?

Just this.

Will he forget who I am? Will he forget my children?

Just this. Just this. Just this.

I remember the pain of anticipation. My beloved uncle was diagnosed with leukemia when I was a medical student. I remember when my aunt called me from the ER. Maybe it was just a severe sinus infection, I told her. But the fear had already set into my bones and so did the anticipation. High fever, an unresolving infection, an exponentially high white blood cell count . . . of course he had cancer, I had thought. I remember being instantly overcome with the anticipation of his possible death.

I felt the same anticipation sitting with my father, and it was excruciating. In fact, it seemed unbearable. In my catastrophic fantasies, I was living out the potential devastation *over and over and over again.*

Just this. I breathed again.

Presence would be my only solace, my only comfort.

My thoughts returned to Scarlett. I am always hesitant about self-disclosure. I don't want to take away from my patients' experience by interjecting my own. And in regard to Scarlett, I did not want to equate the fate of her son, who would likely die young, to my father, who despite an unfortunate diagnosis had the opportunity of a full and meaningful life. But for some reason, I felt compelled to share, and so I did, carefully.

After I shared my story briefly, I told Scarlett, "*Just this.* Just this."

Fortunately, it resonated. Scarlett had come to see me because she was in need of understanding of her difficulty as a mother and as a caretaker. I offered her resources, including a referral to a colleague who taught mindfulness meditation to parents living with children with debilitating disease. She decided to participate in the group and found it to be a much-needed source of comfort and support as well as a helpful resource in cultivating presence in the midst of difficulty. And it was in this context that Scarlett began to address years of worry and a hunger for presence.

HUNGRY
FOR EQUANIMITY

It was in April of 2020 when the global pandemic had locked down the world in quarantine when I had my first telemedicine appointment with David, a long-time patient of mine, and he was scared. While we had worked together for years, he hadn't yet made significant headway. His work as a publicist made it difficult to find time for his own care, and his longstanding anxiety had resulted in unhealthy coping mechanisms. But at that point he was motivated by fear. David was obese, diabetic, hypertensive, precisely the demographic most susceptible to the virulent virus. But while he was motivated, he was also too anxious and overwhelmed. David was dealing with an uncertain crisis as we all were. He had also been dealing with multiple stressors at work and home and just weeks before the pandemic had moved his mother out of her apartment and into a nursing home in New York, where all eyes were nervously watching this crisis unfold with reports of devastating numbers of deaths. Without a doubt, David was dealing with a lot. I could appreciate that moment for how important it was. David has always been at risk and would have benefited from weight loss long ago, but the present circumstances certainly brought that risk into the forefront, and he was eager for change.

But he was overwhelmed by the circumstances, too overwhelmed, he felt, to focus on his wish to improve his health.

Our brains are wired to notice danger in very predictable ways but are not able to discern danger. Traffic, work stress, and tigers are all perceived by our brain in the same way, triggering an acute response that ensures survival, a sympathetic fight or flight response. Acute response to an acute stress is intended to make us act, to flee and remove ourselves from danger. The same response that ensured the survival of our predecessors when they were confronted by danger in the wild is the response that is triggered by modern stress, both acute and chronic. Our modern stressors, while significant, are usually not acute life-and-death stress. Nagging kids are not life-and-death stress. Missed project deadlines are not life-and-death stress. Even the worry over our health and the health of our loved ones in the midst of a pandemic, while justified, is not life-and-death stress, and it certainly is not acute, and yet it is met with the same response, as a trigger to act.

I could identify with the desire to act. My natural response to any crisis is to jump in and do something. And given that I had been fairly resourceful, this reactivity had been rewarded. But I had also reached a point, like David, in which the circumstances were too overwhelming to act and frankly too much out of my control. I had reached the point in which there was no fixing, no fixing my dad, no fixing the pandemic, no fixing the social injustice or the political turmoil that we were facing in the midst of an already difficult time. Despite the triggers, I couldn't act. Despite the stress, I couldn't flee, so what was left?

Understanding this primitive response to stress, we require a high degree of awareness to prevent ourselves from being triggered in the predictable and physiologically explicable way. This awareness is the first step to equanimity, an ability to be with what is, in a non-reactive and balanced way, a state of composure that exists irrespective of external influences and circumstances. Equanimity employs not only presence but also acceptance and empathy toward ourselves and toward others. Equanimity is perceived as a virtue in many ancient traditions, including Hinduism and Buddhism. In these traditions, equanimity is perceived as a balanced positioning, the absence of over-attachment to upheaval, successes, or failures. The act of non-reactivity may be misconceived as indifference, but, in fact, it requires a great deal of compassion, empathy, and restraint. Of course, equanimity is counter to our natural responses and is a practice that must be cultivated, and as these traditions teach, it is a practice that can be cultivated through meditation.

Meditation refers to a set of practices intended to promote emotional regulation and wellbeing through focused attention. Meditation can take on two forms: focused attention meditation, which directs concentration toward an object, such as a body part, the mind, or on an external object, and open monitoring meditation, in which one's attention is directed toward thoughts, emotions, or sensations that arise moment to moment without attaching to or fixating on them. Most meditation practices are a combination of both. Meditation helps focus attention, enhance emotional regulation, and avoid excessive attachments to thoughts, feelings, and experiences. Studies show that meditation does this by literally rewiring the circuitry of the brain in what has been termed neuroplasticity. It was believed that the brain could change and grow only in childhood; however, neuroscientists have since shown that neural networks continue to grow and reorganize well into adulthood. Neuroplasticity refers to the creation of new brain cells or neurons and/or the development of new connections within the brain. Meditation results in structural changes in the brain, specifically in the areas involved in self-awareness, emotional regulation, reactivity, and problem solving.

Neuroimaging studies like functional MRI (fMRI), which not only show the structure of the brain but also record brain activity, have demonstrated these brain changes to occur with meditation.

For example, in a 2012 Harvard study, subjects who participated in an 8-week course in mindfulness-based cognitive therapy (MBCT) demonstrated structural changes in the brain and in brain activity by fMRI in the amygdala, the area of the brain responsible for emotional regulation, even when they were not meditating and were performing normal daily activities. This has been replicated in many other studies since. Other studies have also shown meditation to alter brain activity in the anterior cingulate cortex, the area of the brain responsible for self-regulation and adaptive behavior; the insula, the part of the brain involved in interoception, which is defined as our ability to sense our body's internal states, both conscious and unconscious; as well as the prefrontal cortex, the part of the brain involved in rumination, the process that engages us to continuously think about the same thoughts.

Taken together, these studies have shown that meditation can structurally change and strengthen the areas of the brain that are important to emotional regulation, reactivity, and mood, all of which facilitate equanimity. Meditation practice has also been shown to reduce anxiety, depression, and mood disorders as well as emotional and binge eating, cravings, and body image disturbances. Meditation, therefore, helps facilitate a healthy mindset around food, eating, and body image. Finally, meditation has been associated with health parameters such as reduced blood pressure, all of which made meditation particularly relevant to David's care. Engaging in a meditation practice, I hoped, would help foster a sense of equanimity and allow him to balance his overall concerns with a commitment to his wellbeing.

David returned for a telemedicine visit 3 months later. He had started meditating with an online community and found it so helpful that he was meditating on his own for an hour a day. He had also started a daily walking regimen with his wife. This routine made him more mindful of his diet, and he began to give up some of his most entrenched habits—soda, sweets, and late-night snacking. Most notably, he had almost completely given up Ativan, which he had previously been using daily for anxiety and sleep. Despite his longstanding history of anxiety and the intensified stress of the current circumstances, I found him more at ease than in all those years I had known him. David agreed. He continued his practice, and by the end of the year had lost over 65 pounds. It seemed that amid this adversity, and perhaps because of it, David had finally managed his anxiety and his hunger for equanimity once and for all.

HUNGRY
FOR BALANCE

SHAY AND I HAVE worked together for a long time. Over the course
of our many years together, we've had good days and bad days,
good weeks and bad weeks, and good months and bad months.
Regardless, we are always right back where we started—not just
in terms of weight but in terms of habits. His pendulum swings so
widely that at any given visit his weight can be 15 pounds up or 20
pounds down. His weight loss is never modest, nor is his regain.
Shay lives at the extremes. He will have weeks of consuming only
chicken breasts and salad (even for breakfast) and weeks when he
is eating out three meals a day, including desserts and cocktails.

Balance, I try to preach, but I know that is easier said than done.

I can remember my own pendulum. There were times in my
young life when all I could do was indulge, no *gorge*, on sweets. I
remember in elementary school when I ate an entire box of chocolate bars I was meant to sell for a school fundraiser. I can't quite
remember how I managed to pay the $36 that it cost. I also remem-
ber as an adult being so restrictive that I would eat nothing but
hard-boiled eggs for days. I was so intent on not putting anything
caloric to my lips that I skipped out on tasting my kid's birthday
cake, as well as my own, and subsisted at times on just a spoon of
peanut butter before heading out on a long run—whether I was

planning to run 10 miles or 16. Extremes were easier than balance for me. I had trouble inhabiting the middle ground, and I find this is the case in many of my patients as well.

Of course, middle ground is hard and takes work. It requires managing the tension that pulls us toward the extremes. It certainly is easier, in a way, to live at extremes. It requires less thought, less intention, and less compromise. Our struggle with middle ground is not limited to food, of course; we are by human nature black and white, good or bad, right or wrong. But extremes are not consistent with living in equilibrium. As I have become more aware of this tendency for extremes in myself and in my patients, I find it plays out everywhere and heavily in the practice of medicine.

In my role as medical director of the center for weight loss, I collaborated closely with my surgical colleagues who performed weight loss surgery. In our center, the treatment of obesity was a continuum, which included behavioral modification, medications, and bariatric surgery for whom it was appropriate. But I often found that many physicians and health care providers did not have the flexibility to understand and engage in this scope of care. Medical doctors didn't *believe* in surgery, and surgeons did not believe in medical therapy. Behavioral therapists recommend intuitive eating at the exclusion of effective medical treatments while some doctors and surgeons refused to acknowledge the many emotional *hungers*, focusing narrowly on physiology. This type of either/or thinking was always to the detriment of patients who were swayed away from considering all possible options for their care.

I see the same dichotomy between Eastern and Western medicine and between traditional versus holistic or integrative practices. In reality there is a need for both. There is a time when only antibiotics can treat a raging pneumonia or pyelonephritis and other times when only connection and nature can provide healing.

We are all served best when we can draw from the extremes in order to navigate the middle road.

Shay returned to see me after a not so unusual hiatus. But this time it was different. Since our previous visit, he had an episode of overindulgence, and as a result he had his first episode of gout—an excruciating and debilitating inflammation of the joint that is usually prompted by an overindulgence of food. Foods such as meat and alcohol that contain high amounts of uric acid can precipitate a gouty attack. Uric acid is processed and cleared by the kidneys as urine. However, in gout, the amount of uric acid overwhelms the body's capacity to clear it, resulting in crystal formation in the joints, often the big toe, which presents as a red, swollen, inflamed and exquisitely tender joint sensitive to even the sensation of a bed sheet. While this condition is treatable and temporary, it can be recurrent, and for Shay, knowing that was enough. His fear of a recurrent attack was enough to force him to find balance in his ways. That is when our work together truly began. It is not to say that it was easy or even necessarily consistent, but at least we could operate from an intention of balance as opposed to a practice of compensating extreme indulgence with over-restriction, a pattern of punishing and rewarding.

Human nature gravitates toward extremes, but our relationship with food provides an opportunity to exercise balance. Given the nature of food as both essential and non-essential, necessary, but with the potential to tempt us to excess, the choice in how we nourish ourselves is an opportunity in exercising the middle ground. In my experience, navigating this balance opens our minds to broader change in our lives. This, for me, is the greatest beauty in this work.

HUNGRY
FOR MEANING

When I first met Sherry, she could barely get herself into my office. It took her several minutes of maneuvering from her wheelchair to her walker and from her walker to the office chair. Once there it took several more minutes for her to get comfortable. When she finally settled, she was breathing heavily, and I could see beads of sweat lining her forehead. Her painstaking effort at mobility showed her conviction, and I could imagine the enterprising entrepreneur she had once been.

Sherry shared with me how she created a product line and established a multimillion-dollar company as a result. I could not help but raise my eyebrows as she rattled off the very skincare products I had sitting in my medicine cabinet. An abundance of success came to a halt when she was diagnosed with lupus. That year came also with the loss of her mobility; the loss of her husband, who divorced her because he was unable to tolerate her new disability; the loss of her businesses; and, finally, the loss of her wealth and financial freedom. Her entire life, all that she had worked for, was taken away, just like that. As a result, she lost her will, her drive, and her sense of purpose. Sherry described that over the following decade she slowly morphed into a person she no longer knew. With the 120-pound weight gain that ensued came greater disability, bitterness, self-loathing, and loss of self.

"I don't even know who I am anymore," Sherry said. "I am so far from that person I used to be."

When I asked her why she had come to see me then, she answered in the most vulnerable and authentic way I have ever heard from a patient.

"Because I deserve more. I deserve more than self-pity. I deserve more than self-loathing. Because," she said as she looked down to her hands, "I deserve to live a life with meaning."

Vulnerable yet laced with a knowing that was so hopeful. It was not often that I met a patient with such keen awareness, who was able to articulate it with such clarity. Sure, they know that they want to lose weight, but why? That part usually requires more unpacking.

I always begin a new-patient evaluation with "Why are you here?" Often, the patient will stare back at me, perplexed. The answer should be obvious: "To lose weight, of course."

"But *why* do you want to lose weight?" I ask.

"Because I want to fit into my wedding band."

"Because I want to run a 5K."

"Because I want run around and play ball with my kid."

All these reasons, while personal, are still skimming the surface of the true, deep intentions of why they are here with me, now.

Sometimes, the embedded value seems clear. For example, people often reach out after a new diagnosis, such as diabetes or high blood pressure. The value here is health or vitality. Other times, the new diagnosis prompts a desire to become healthy for a partner, for a child or grandchild. While there is a value here for family and relationship, it still neglects that deep and personal intention, the true reason for wanting change.

Each of us has an intention that emanates from the deepest, truest part of us, that motivates us to live our life to our fullest potential. That deep knowing can be referred to as our soul, spirit, blueprint, essence, north star, guiding light, or true self. Whatever you wish to call it, there is an intuition that exists in the deepest part of our being which encapsulates our values, our principles, our passion, our purpose, and our will to meaning. This deep knowing is our personal wellspring of wisdom that will steer us to meet our greatest potential if we allow it. It provides the guidance to align our intentions with our actions and to show up as the best version of ourselves, and this alignment is what brings us our greatest joy and fulfillment.

But while this knowing is intuitive, it does not mean that we arrive at this understanding without work or struggle. Just because we deserve a fulfilled and contented life does not mean we can achieve it with ease. This is because this intuitive part of us is hidden. It gets hidden by beliefs and stories, titles and status, expectations, missteps, misunderstandings, misgivings, and all the other baggage that is accumulated over the course of a lifetime. Uncluttering our minds and uncovering the deep-seated *why* requires self-examination, introspection, soul-searching, and self-actualization. And this is an arduous and often painful task. It takes work. But it is worth the work because with it comes clarity, the clarity that allows us to pursue our path with self-assuredness and conviction, work that leads us to a life well lived. Alternatively, lack of clarity will impede our success. Lack of awareness will drive us to superficial goals and superficial and short-term successes. In order to engage in this deep, meaningful, and often painful work, we must acknowledge that we are worthy of the work and worthy of the effort that is required. This is a prerequisite and necessary requirement for this change and the primary stumbling block in this journey. Knowing that we are worthy of the undeniable effort required to fulfill a life of intention and meaning.

Sherry's response to my question articulates the knowing that she is worthy. She is worthy of a life in which she respects and values herself. She is worthy of a life free from self-pity, self-loathing, and self-contempt. And she is worthy of the effort required to show that self-respect and care for herself. This awareness is powerful and drives the conviction and assuredness that is necessary for transformative change.

So, when my patients tell me that they want to fit into their wedding band or run a 5K or run around with their kids, I dig deeper. I want more. More understanding. More unraveling. More depth to uncover the true reason they are seeking change. Under all the hidden layers, there lies a knowing of that which they hold dear, of their sense of purpose and their mission, that which gives them meaning and fulfillment. As I start to peel back the layers, patients begin to reveal their core values, the *why* that has prompted them to seek a different way of being.

These revelations, in my experience, are essential to identifying the true hunger, the hunger to find meaning. This is a necessary and essential exercise. Whether someone suffers from excess weight or not, suffers a disability or not, has endured trauma, grief, and pain or not, is falling apart or appears to have their lives seamlessly orchestrated—we are all searching for meaning. In fact, we are *starving* for meaning, the basic human need to find purpose and significance in our lives.

Poets and mystics across the ages have deliberated this yearning. Victor Frankl described the human desire to find meaning as *the* very guiding principle of our lives. In *Man's Search for Meaning*— part memoir of his personal experiences in the Holocaust, part introduction of *logotherapy*, the school of psychotherapy he founded that centered on meaning—Dr. Frankl writes that what drives man's purpose is his "will-to-meaning," and this can be realized in three ways. The first is through our life's achievements. The second is in how we love. And the third, and perhaps the most poignant, is in how we suffer. Dr. Frankl describes through his lived experiences in Auschwitz that even in the worst circumstances, we can find meaning, and out of our pain and suffering we can create significance. Herein lies a choice, he instructs, the uniquely human potential to challenge ourselves and to persevere.

Sherry's suffering did just that. In enduring the loss, the pain, and the suffering, she arrived at an understanding, a choice to create meaning out of her experiences and to pursue a new way of living that honored her innermost values.

So began my relationship with Sherry. Sometimes, it would take a week for her to lose 2 to 3 pounds. Other times it would take a month. But she lost weight steadily. Some weeks, like the anniversary of her marriage or the anniversary of her diagnosis, she would experience a setback. These setbacks were met with such heartache. But ultimately, she held her heartbreak with understanding and self-compassion, and this is what allowed her to continue.

Sherry did not need to be told that she needed to persevere despite hardship—she was intimately aware of this fact. And she never forgot her choice to create a new narrative. There, she had an opportunity to meet the inevitable stumbling blocks with resilience, to persist despite difficulty to achieve the beauty on the other side.

She accepted this invitation. Over the course of the 2 and a half years we worked together, Sherry lost over 150 pounds and, despite her disability, has kept it off over 10 years later. Remarkably, through intense physical therapy and sheer grit, Sherry regained her mobility and was able to ambulate without her wheelchair. And at the time of this writing, Sherry has started a new company, an online program that guides entrepreneurs to create a sustainable business with purpose. She tells me she starts every class by asking people to identify their why.

People often ask me why I chose this career, why I specialized in weight loss. I never have a good answer. Sometimes, I wander into the convoluted story about how I got pregnant before my GI fellowship and was forced to pivot. Other times, I share my fascination behind the science of obesity medicine and the fact that something so topical fulfilled my love of data and evidence-based medicine. Maybe it had to do with my upbringing and the fact that food was so intricately intertwined with my family culture and traditions. And of course, I would be remiss not to acknowledge my own personal battle with weight and body image, one that overshadowed so much of my childhood and young adult life. Certainly, this work allowed me to heal those wounds, which, looking back now with a doctor's eye, were so injurious to my psyche and, looking back with a mother's eye, were just so unfortunate and unkind.

Sherry taught me the power of the human spirit and human potential. She taught me what is possible when one is truly clear and aligned with their deepest values. This potential to find meaning, for connecting with what gives us joy and fulfillment, is inherent and exists in all of us. As Sherry's experiences exemplify, it is hard, but it is because of this hardship that we are forced to uncover and reconcile our true values. This should not be seen as a hindrance but an invitation. Therein lies the work. Our uniquely personal work to uncover the values that motivate us to carry out our lives in a way that is in accordance with what we hold dear. It is our birthright. To find meaning in our lives is the antidote to the void, to the emptiness, and to the *hunger* we are all seeking to fill.

Sitting here now, as I reflect on the events and experiences that have led me to this point in time, I cannot feel anything but gratitude. Gratitude for the arc of my life's experiences that has brought me here. For the experience of every hunger I have witnessed in my patients and the recognition that I, too, have experienced each and every hunger myself. While we are unique, our experiences are universal. My role as a doctor has afforded me the privilege of understanding this truth. As a recipient of these stories, I have come to recognize that the patterns in my patients' experiences are universal and human. I know now that these experiences, however challenging, were a prerequisite, a priming to my own will-to-meaning, to identifying my unique purpose, and an opportunity to fulfill *my* own hunger.

Epilogue:
Just Hungry

Emily is a content editor and marketing strategist for a budding startup in the health and wellness space. She is charismatic, focused, and determined but also disheartened. She has never had a "weight problem," but the transition of the past few years from student to worker-bee has resulted in less time for self-care, frequent meals outside the home, lack of exercise, and weight gain. Emily tells me that she has tried multiple diets over the past year to reverse this trend, but none have helped her lose weight.

"I'm just too hungry!" she says.

"Give me an example," I ask. "Are you *dieting* now?"

She nods yes.

"So, what's the first thing you eat when you wake up?"

"I try not to eat in the morning," she says. "But by lunchtime I am starving! So, I eat a salad."

"What's in it?" I ask.

"Lettuce, tomatoes, other random veggies. Sometimes I add in an egg white."

"That's it?" I ask.

She nods again.

"Does that fill you up?" I ask.

She shakes her head side to side vigorously and looks at me wide eyed as if to communicate a shared surprise.

"Then what do you eat?"

Basically, Emily will make do with some carrots, a rice cake or a slice of turkey. By dinnertime she is "really starving." She eats another salad, maybe with some chicken. But she is still hungry. She tries to ignore her hunger but most times she will break down and raid the pantry or fridge and eat *everything in sight* until she is finally full.

Other times, she will grit her teeth for days before she hits her breaking point. But, invariably, she breaks down. And she is so frustrated by this.

"See!" she says. "I'm just too hungry!"

"So," I say, "you starve yourself all day, sometimes for days, and then you are surprised to find that you are hungry?"

Nearly every patient who has come into the office has shared a similar experience at some point in time and also has shared a similar surprise. As if it should be surprising that one feels hungry when they are kept hungry. Not that I don't understand, I do. I cannot count how many times I starved myself, ignoring my hunger, only to be frustrated and angered that my hunger would not bend to my will. But our hunger will not bend just because we wish it so. As we have discussed, there is actually an intricate physiology that dictates our hunger.

Our bodies have an elaborate system of hormones and neural signals that inform our brains of nutrient status and our hunger. Our gut, stomach and intestines, pancreas, and fat cells all release hormones that converge on appetite centers in the hypothalamus and are further integrated in higher brain centers to determine whether we are hungry or full. These hormonal signals fall into two categories, those that signal hunger, such as ghrelin, and those that signal energy sufficiency, such as GLP-1 (glucagon-like peptide 1), PYY (peptide tyrosine tyrosine), CCK (cholecystokinin), and leptin. Insulin and glucose also signal energy sufficiency to the brain. As we have discussed, ghrelin levels steadily rise before meals, signaling hunger and are suppressed after food intake then slowly begin to rise again. There is a very predictable rise and fall of ghrelin around mealtimes.

GLP-1, on the other hand, is released from the small intestine within minutes of food ingestion and again later when food travels down and reaches the small intestine. Once the intestines "sense" nutrients, GLP-1 and PYY rise in a coordinated response that signals fullness to the brain. Longer-term energy signals also exist, such as leptin, which come from adipocytes, or fat cells. In contrast to the other hormones mentioned, which respond to short-term nutrient intake, leptin exists in relation to the amount of fat stored in the cell and therefore is a long-term energy signal. The greater the fat accumulation in a cell, the greater release of leptin. This makes sense because the excess storage of calories as fat is being relayed to the brain as a signal to eat less.

When we do not eat, as in fasting, satiety cues get dysregulated. For example, leptin and GLP-1 decrease with fasting, creating more hunger. And ghrelin levels increase, as does ghrelin receptor activity, meaning that the body becomes even more sensitive to the hunger signal of ghrelin. So, to be clear, when we fast or starve, we invariably feel greater hunger, and this is mediated by our hunger hormones. It should go without saying that when we allow ourselves to get hungry, *we get hungry*, and this hunger is physiologic.

There is an alternative to fasting, which is to eat properly. Our hunger cues respond to a proper balance of macronutrients. For example, protein will suppress ghrelin levels to a greater degree than carbohydrates, which will more effectively suppress ghrelin than a high-in-fat meal. Additionally, a higher-protein breakfast will result in a higher level of GLP-1 throughout the day and has been shown to reduce overall food intake, including snacking. So, a more effective strategy of losing weight is managing hunger (and hunger hormones) by eating properly, not by avoiding food, instigating our hunger, and ultimately undermining our weight loss goals.

Energy homeostasis, however, is complicated. When we restrict calories and lose weight, our hunger hormones will shift in a manner that will promote more hunger. I mentioned that leptin levels correlate with the amount of fat stored in the adipocyte. While greater fat results in greater leptin secretion, the converse of this is also true. Less fat or the loss of fat through calorie restriction will reduce leptin secretion, signaling *less* fullness or, said another way, more hunger.

The same is true for ghrelin, GLP-1, PYY, CCK, and other hormones which shift in response to weight loss in a manner that triggers greater hunger. So, while I encourage my patients to honor their hunger rather than avoid it, I also want them to learn to sit with the feeling without reacting when they know that they are adequately nourished. These two concepts are not mutually exclusive or in opposition to each other. Nourishing ourselves properly and knowing we have done so allows us to sit with this feeling of hunger without reacting.

Hunger does trigger us to react. When blood sugar drops, the first response by the body is to release adrenaline. Adrenaline, also called epinephrine, is the stress hormone that is released when the body senses danger. Adrenaline stimulates the fight or flight response of the body, increasing heart rate and blood pressure, directing blood flow to the muscles, and preparing the body for action. Adrenaline also ensures that the body keeps running by mobilizing glucose stores as an energy source for the brain so that it can continue to function in a time of perceived starvation.

While hunger does trigger us to react, as a survival mechanism to mitigate starvation, it is useful to remember that not all hunger is starvation. While the feeling of hunger is uncomfortable and stimulates our body's stress response, in most cases, we are not in danger, particularly if we have adequately nourished ourselves. This is not of course, the case with Emily, who essentially has been alternating between starving and bingeing.

Certainly, hunger can represent a true need for food, but the feeling of hunger can be triggered by other things as well. As we have discussed, thoughts, emotions, sights, smells, and other food cues will also trigger hunger that is not a true physiologic need for food. And weight loss, which may in fact be necessary for one's health, may also stimulate hunger. Knowing this may help us manage the body's response to healthy weight loss. The realization that we are not in danger when hunger strikes can help us manage the anxious response that it triggers. This understanding also allows us to pause, to sit with the feeling of hunger and ask the necessary question, "Am I *really* hungry?" A healthy diet should not leave you hungry all the time or make you feel as if you are *starving*. But a healthy diet may still leave you with cravings or feelings of hunger as you try to navigate a different way of nourishing yourself. If you are used to snacking excessively or eating portions so large that you feel overly full, scaling back on meal size or avoiding snacks between meals can leave you with a hunger or desire to eat that does not necessarily need to be responded to. While it may feel as if your body is telling you that you need to eat, it is this kind of eating that may have resulted in excess weight to begin with. So, if you know you have consumed enough food, it is ok to sit with this feeling of desire without allowing the anxiety to overtake you. Being comfortable with the uncomfortable feeling of hunger allows you to evaluate the sensation, examine it, and to respond in a way that is consistent with what your body really needs. With time, your body will adapt too.

I encourage Emily to pay attention to her hunger. To honor her hunger by nourishing herself properly without fasting and starving. But also understanding that a time may come when her hunger might not represent a true need for nutrients. This should be noted as Emily navigates a new relationship with food. It seems easy, but I know that it is not, and it is a difficult concept for Emily to grasp. We set out on an exercise. I ask her to explore her hunger. I ask her to notice her hunger as she modifies the way she eats. How does her hunger change if she eats slowly? How does it change when she eats processed carbohydrates as compared to balanced meals high in protein? Does skipping meals affect her hunger and her ability to feel full? I also ask her to notice how she feels if she stops eating just before she feels really full. Sometimes, it's a matter of just one bite, that one bite that becomes too much. Does she find that even in those moments, if she waits, that invariably her sensation of *not yet full* subsides? Emily has never really explored her hunger in this way. After engaging in this practice for several months, Emily notices that food is so much more satisfying when she responds to her hunger properly. As often is the case, our hunger is varied, diverse, and presents in unique ways, but our hunger is also universal. Learning to recognize our hunger is a process, a journey that will unfold in remarkable and awe-inspiring ways, but only if we let it.

CITATIONS

Introduction
Eger, E. E., Weigand, E. S., & Zimbardo, P. G. (2017). *The choice: Embrace the possible.* New York: Scribner.

Moberg, K. (2013). Oxytocin effects in mothers and infants during breastfeeding. *Infant, 9*(6), 201-206.

Hungry for Self-Compassion
Burnette, J. L., & Finkel, E. J. (2012). Buffering against weight gain following dieting setbacks: An implicit theory intervention. *Journal of Experimental Social Psychology, 48*(3), 721-725. doi:10.1016/j.jesp.2011.12.020

Frost, R. O., Marten, P., Lahart, C., & Rosenblate, R. (1990). The dimensions of perfectionism. *Cognitive Therapy and Research, 14*(5), 449-468. doi:10.1007/bf01172967

Mantzios, M., & Wilson, J. (2013). Making concrete construals mindful: A novel approach for developing mindfulness and self-compassion to assist weight loss. *Psychology & Health, 29*(4), 422-441. doi:10.1080/08870446.2013.863883

Sirois, F. M. (2015). A self-regulation resource model of self-compassion and health behavior intentions in emerging adults. *Preventive Medicine Reports, 2*, 218-222. doi:10.1016/j.pmedr.2015.03.006

Stoeber, J., Lalova, A. V., & Lumley, E. J. (2020). Perfectionism, (self-)compassion, and subjective well-being: A mediation model. *Personality and Individual Differences, 154*, 109708. doi:10.1016/j.paid.2019.109708

Hungry for Self-Love

Diagnostic and statistical manual of mental disorders: DSM-5. (2017). Arlington, VA: American Psychiatric Association.

Kearney-Cooke, A., & Tieger, D. (2015). Body image disturbance and the development of eating disorders. *The Wiley Handbook of Eating Disorders*, 283-296. doi:10.1002/9781118574089.ch22

Kohl, H., & Cook, H. (2013). Read "educating the student BODY: Taking physical activity and physical education to school" at NAP.edu. Retrieved April 07, 2021, from https://www.nap.edu/read/18314/chapter/1

Lichtman, S., & Poser, E. G. (1983). The effects of exercise on mood and cognitive functioning. *Journal of Psychosomatic Research, 27*(1), 43-52. doi:10.1016/0022-3999(83)90108-3

Marques, A., Hillman, C., & Sardinha, L. (2018). Physical activity, aerobic fitness and academic achievement. *Health and Academic Achievement.* doi:10.5772/intechopen.71284

Naidoo, U. (2020). *This is your brain on food: An indispensable guide to the surprising foods that fight depression, anxiety, PTSD, OCD, ADHD, and more.* New York: Little, Brown Spark.

Pearl, R. L., Wadden, T. A., Hopkins, C. M., Shaw, J. A., Hayes, M. R., Bakizada, Z. M., . . . Alamuddin, N. (2017). Association between weight bias internalization and metabolic syndrome among treatment-seeking individuals with obesity. *Obesity, 25*(2), 317-322. doi:10.1002/oby.21716

Puhl RM, Heuer CA. (2009). The stigma of obesity: A review and update. *Obesity,* 17(5), 941-64. doi: 10.1038/oby.2008.636.2009.19165161.

Sutin, A. R., Stephan, Y., & Terracciano, A. (2015). Weight discrimination and risk of mortality. *Psychological Science, 26*(11), 1803-1811. doi:10.1177/0956797615601103

Trudeau, F., & Shephard, R. J. (2008). Physical education, school physical activity, school sports and academic performance. *International Journal of Behavioral Nutrition and Physical Activity, 5*(1), 10. doi:10.1186/1479-5868-5-10

Vogel, L. (2019). Fat shaming is making people sicker and heavier. *Canadian Medical Association Journal, 191*(23). doi:10.1503/cmaj.109-5758

Hungry for Routine
Arlinghaus, K. R., & Johnston, C. A. (2018). The importance of creating habits and routine. *American Journal of Lifestyle Medicine, 13*(2), 142-144. doi:10.1177/1559827618818044

Gardner, B., Lally, P., & Wardle, J. (2012). Making health habitual: The psychology of "habit-formation" and general practice. *British Journal of General Practice, 62*(605), 664-666. doi:10.3399/bjgp12x659466

Neal, D. T., Wood, W., Labrecque, J. S., & Lally, P. (2012). How do habits guide behavior? Perceived and actual triggers of habits in daily life. *Journal of Experimental Social Psychology, 48*(2), 492-498. doi:10.1016/j.jesp.2011.10.011

Hungry for Abundance

Bays, H., & Scinta, W. (2015). Adiposopathy and epigenetics: An introduction to obesity as a transgenerational disease. *Current Medical Research and Opinion, 31*(11), 2059-2069. doi: 10.1185/03007995.2015.1087983

Martins, V. J., Toledo Florêncio, T. M., Grillo, L. P., Do Carmo P. Franco, M., Martins, P. A., Clemente, A. P., . . . Sawaya, A. L. (2011). Long-lasting effects of undernutrition. *International Journal of Environmental Research and Public Health, 8*(6), 1817-1846. doi:10.3390/ijerph8061817

Mühlhäusler, B. S., Adam, C. L., & McMillen, I. C. (2008). Maternal nutrition and the programming of obesity. *Organogenesis, 4*(3), 144-152. doi:10.4161/org.4.3.6503

Painter, R., De Rooij, S., Osmond, C., Gluckman, P., Hanson, M., Phillips, D., & Roseboom, T. (2009). Transgenerational effects of prenatal exposure to the Dutch famine. *BJOG: An International Journal of Obstetrics & Gynaecology, 116*(6), 868-868. doi:10.1111/j.1471-0528.2009.02108.x

Painter, R., Osmond, C., Gluckman, P., Hanson, M., Phillips, D., & Roseboom, T. (2008). Transgenerational effects of prenatal exposure to the Dutch famine on NEONATAL adiposity and health in later life. *BJOG: An International Journal of Obstetrics & Gynaecology, 115*(10), 1243-1249. doi:10.1111/j.1471-0528.2008.01822.x

Roseboom, T. J. (2000). Coronary heart disease after prenatal exposure to the dutch famine, 1944-45. *Heart, 84*(6), 595-598. doi:10.1136/heart.84.6.595

Sumithran, P., Prendergast, L. A., Delbridge, E., Purcell, K., Shulkes, A., Kriketos, A., & Proietto, J. (2011). Long-term persistence of hormonal adaptations to weight loss. *New England Journal of Medicine, 365*(17), 1597-1604. doi:10.1056/nejmoa1105816

Hungry for Nature

Berman, M. G., Jonides, J., & Kaplan, S. (2008). The cognitive benefits of interacting with nature. *Psychological Science, 19*(12), 1207-1212. doi:10.1111/j.1467-9280.2008.02225.x

Faber Taylor, A., & Kuo, F. E. (2009). Children with attention deficits concentrate better after walk in the park. *Journal of Attention Disorders, 12*(5), 402-409. doi:10.1177/1087054708323000

Shin, W. S., Shin, C. S., Yeoun, P. S., & Kim, J. J. (2011). The influence of interaction with forest on cognitive function. *Scandinavian Journal of Forest Research, 26*(6), 595-598. doi:10.1080/02827581.2011.585996

Twohig-Bennett, C., & Jones, A. (2018). The health benefits of the great outdoors: A systematic review and meta-analysis of greenspace exposure and health outcomes. *Environmental Research, 166,* 628-637. doi:10.1016/j.envres.2018.06.030

Ulrich, R. S., Simons, R. F., Losito, B. D., Fiorito, E., Miles, M. A., & Zelson, M. (1991). Stress recovery during exposure to natural and urban environments. *Journal of Environmental Psychology, 11*(3), 201-230. doi:10.1016/s0272-4944(05)80184-7

Hungry for Belonging
Klok, M. D., Jakobsdottir, S., & Drent, M. L. (2007). The role of leptin and ghrelin in the regulation of food intake and body weight in humans: A review. *Obesity Reviews, 8*(1), 21-34. doi:10.1111/j.1467-789x.2006.00270.x

Schellekens, H., Finger, B. C., Dinan, T. G., & Cryan, J. F. (2012). Ghrelin signalling and obesity: At the interface of stress, mood and food reward. *Pharmacology & Therapeutics, 135*(3), 316-326. doi:10.1016/j.pharmthera.2012.06.004

Stanley, S., Wynne, K., McGowan, B., & Bloom, S. (2005). Hormonal regulation of food intake. *Physiological Reviews, 85*(4), 1131-1158. doi:10.1152/physrev.00015.2004

Hungry for Self-Acceptance
Gross, J. J., & John, O. P. (2003). Individual differences in two emotion regulation processes: Implications for AFFECT, relationships, and well-being. *Journal of Personality and Social Psychology, 85*(2), 348-362. doi:10.1037/0022-3514.85.2.348

Kivity, Y., Tamir, M., & Huppert, J. D. (2016). Self-acceptance of negative emotions: The positive relationship with effective cognitive reappraisal. *International Journal of Cognitive Therapy, 9*(4), 279-294. doi:10.1521/ijct_2016_09_10

Lazarus, R. S., & Alfert, E. (1964). Short-circuiting of threat by experimentally altering cognitive appraisal. *The Journal of Abnormal and Social Psychology, 69*(2), 195-205. doi:10.1037/h0044635

Ryff, C. D. (1989). Happiness is everything, or is it? Explorations on the meaning of psychological well-being. *Journal of Personality and Social Psychology, 57*(6), 1069-1081. doi:10.1037/0022-3514.57.6.1069

Shepard, L. A. (1979). Self-acceptance: The evaluative component of the self-concept construct. *American Educational Research Journal, 16*(2), 139-160. doi:10.3102/00028312016002139

Hungry for Ritual
Chavez, A. (2018). *Amy's Guide to Best Behavior in Japan: Do It Right and Be Polite!* Stone Bridge Press.

Hammons, A. J., & Fiese, B. H. (2011). Is frequency of shared family meals related to the nutritional health of children and adolescents? *Pediatrics, 127*(6). doi:10.1542/peds.2010-1440

Jewish dietary LAWS (Kashrut): Overview of laws & regulations. (n.d.). Retrieved April 06, 2021,

from https://www.jewishvirtuallibrary.org/
overview-of-jewish-dietary-laws-and-regulations

Lee, H. J., Lee, S. Y., & Park, E. C. (2015). Do family meals affect childhood overweight or obesity? Nationwide Survey 2008-2012. *Pediatric Obesity, 11*(3), 161-165. doi:10.1111/ijpo.12035

Neril, R. (2017, March 27). Sustainable Jewish eating. Retrieved April 06, 2021, from https://www.myjewishlearning.com/article/sustainable-jewish-eating/

Hungry for a Possibility
Suzuki, S. (2011). *Zen Mind, Beginner's Mind: Informal Talks on Zen Meditation and Practice* – June 28, 2011. Boulder,, Colorado: Shambhala.

Hungry for Motivation
Fishbach, A., & Trope, Y. (2005). The substitutability of external control and self-control. *Journal of Experimental Social Psychology, 41*(3), 256-270. doi:10.1016/j.jesp.2004.07.002

Georgiadis, M. M., Biddle, S. J., & Stavrou, N. A. (2006). Motivation for weight-loss diets: A clustering, longitudinal field study using self-esteem and self-determination theory perspectives. *Health Education Journal, 65*(1), 53-72. doi:10.1177/0017896906066067

Gneezy, U., Meier, S., & Rey-Biel, P. (2011). When and why incentives (don't) work to modify behavior. *Journal of Economic Perspectives, 25*(4), 191-210. doi:10.1257/jep.25.4.191

Ryan, R. M., & Deci, E. L. (2000). Self-determination theory and the facilitation of intrinsic motivation, social development, and well-being. American Psychologist, 55, 68–78

Silva, M. N., Vieira, P. N., Coutinho, S. R., Minderico, C. S., Matos, M. G., Sardinha, L. B., & Teixeira, P. J. (2010). Using self-determination theory to promote physical activity and weight control: A randomized controlled trial in women. Journal of Behavioral Medicine, 33(2), 110–122. https://doi.org/10.1007/s10865-009-9239-y

Teixeira, P. J., Silva, M. N., Mata, J., Palmeira, A. L., & Markland, D. (2012). Motivation, self-determination, and long-term weight control. *International Journal of Behavioral Nutrition and Physical Activity, 9*(1), 22. doi:10.1186/1479-5868-9-22

Hungry for Understanding

Eight-year weight losses with an intensive lifestyle intervention: The look ahead study. (2014). *Obesity, 22*(1), 5-13. doi:10.1002/oby.20662

Stotland, S. C., & Larocque, M. (2005). Early treatment response as a predictor of ongoing weight loss in obesity treatment. *British Journal of Health Psychology, 10*(4), 601-614. doi:10.1348/135910705x43750

Treyzon, L., Chen, S., Hong, K., Yan, E., Carpenter, C. L., Thames, G., . . . Li, Z. (2008). A controlled trial of protein enrichment of meal replacements for weight reduction with retention of lean body mass. *Nutrition Journal, 7*(1). doi:10.1186/1475-2891-7-23

Wadden, T. A., Foster, G. D., Wang, J., Pierson, R. N., Yang, M. U., Moreland, K., . . . VanItallie, T. B. (1992). Clinical correlates of short- and long-term weight loss. *The American Journal of Clinical Nutrition, 56*(1). doi:10.1093/ajcn/56.1.271s

Hungry to Heal

Bower-Russa, M. E., Knutson, J. F., & Winebarger, A. (2001). Disciplinary history, adult disciplinary attitudes, and risk for abusive parenting. *Journal of Community Psychology, 29*(3), 219-240. doi:10.1002/jcop.1015

Campbell, J. A., Walker, R. J., & Egede, L. E. (2016). Associations between adverse childhood Experiences, high-risk behaviors, and morbidity in adulthood. *American Journal of Preventive Medicine, 50*(3), 344-352. doi:10.1016/j.amepre.2015.07.022

Felitti, V. (2010). Obesity: Problem, solution, or both? *The Permanente Journal, 14*(1). doi:10.7812/tpp/09-107

Felitti, V. J., Anda, R. F., Nordenberg, D., Williamson, D. F., Spitz, A. M., Edwards, V., . . . Marks, J. S. (1998). Relationship of childhood abuse and household dysfunction to many of the leading causes of death in adults. *American Journal of Preventive Medicine, 14*(4), 245-258. doi:10.1016/s0749-3797(98)00017-8

Gilbert, L. K., Breiding, M. J., Merrick, M. T., Thompson, W. W., Ford, D. C., Dhingra, S. S., & Parks, S. E. (2015). Childhood adversity and adult chronic disease. *American Journal of Preventive Medicine, 48*(3), 345-349. doi:10.1016/j.amepre.2014.09.006

Lynch, B. A., Agunwamba, A., Wilson, P. M., Kumar, S., Jacobson, R. M., Phelan, S., . . . Finney Rutten, L. J. (2016). Adverse family experiences and obesity in children and adolescents in the United States. *Preventive Medicine, 90*, 148-154. doi:10.1016/j.ypmed.2016.06.035

Montalvo-Ortiz, J., Gelernter, J., Wymbs, N., Althoff, R., Hudziak, J., Zhao, H., & Kaufman, J. (2018). 20. Child abuse and epigenetic mechanisms of disease risk. *Biological Psychiatry, 83*(9). doi:10.1016/j.biopsych.2018.02.037

Su, S., Jimenez, M. P., Roberts, C. T., & Loucks, E. B. (2015). The role of adverse childhood experiences in cardiovascular disease risk: A review with emphasis on plausible mechanisms. *Current cardiology reports, 17*(10), 88. https://doi.org/10.1007/s11886-015-0645-1

Williamson, D., Thompson, T., Anda, R., Dietz, W., & Felitti, V. (2002). Body weight and obesity in adults and self-reported abuse in childhood. *International Journal of Obesity, 26*(8), 1075-1082. doi:10.1038/sj.ijo.0802038

Yang, B. (2013). Child abuse and epigenetic mechanisms of disease risk. *American Journal of Preventive Medicine, 44*(2). doi:10.1016/s0749-3797(12)00923-3

Hungry for Movement

Asmundson, G. J., Fetzner, M. G., DeBoer, L. B., Powers, M. B., Otto, M. W., & Smits, J. A. (2013). Let's get physical: A contemporary review of the anxiolytic effects of exercise for anxiety and its disorders. *Depression and Anxiety, 30*(4), 362-373. doi:10.1002/da.22043

Byrne, A., & Byrne, D. (1993). The effect of exercise on depression, anxiety and other mood states: A review. *Journal of Psychosomatic Research, 37*(6), 565-574. doi:10.1016/0022-3999(93)90050-p

Harber, V. J., & Sutton, J. R. (1984). Endorphins and exercise. *Sports Medicine, 1*(2), 154-171. doi:10.2165/00007256-198401020-00004

Netz, Y., & Lidor, R. (2003). Mood alterations in mindful versus aerobic exercise modes. *The Journal of Psychology, 137*(5), 405-419. doi:10.1080/00223980309600624

Hungry for Patience

Blackburn, G. (1995). Effect of degree of weight loss on health benefits. *Obesity Research, 3*(S2). doi:10.1002/j.1550-8528.1995.tb00466.x

Casazza, K., Fontaine, K. R., Astrup, A., Birch, L. L., Brown, A. W., Bohan Brown, M. M., . . . Allison, D. B. (2013). Myths, presumptions, and facts about obesity. *New England Journal of Medicine, 368*(5), 446-454. doi:10.1056/nejmsa1208051

Clark, A., Ledger, W., Galletly, C., Tomlinson, L., Blaney, F., Wang, X., & Norman, R. (1995). Weight loss results in significant improvement in pregnancy and ovulation rates in anovulatory obese women. *Human Reproduction, 10*(10), 2705-2712. doi:10.1093/oxfordjournals.humrep.a135772

Foster, G. D., Wadden, T. A., Vogt, R. A., & Brewer, G. (1997). What is a reasonable weight loss? Patients' expectations and evaluations of obesity treatment outcomes.

Journal of Consulting and Clinical Psychology, 65(1), 79-85. doi.10.1037/0022-000x.05.1.79

Steinberg, D. M., Bennett, G. G., Askew, S., & Tate, D. F. (2015). Weighing every day matters: Daily weighing improves weight loss and adoption of weight control behaviors. *Journal of the Academy of Nutrition and Dietetics, 115*(4), 511-518. doi:10.1016/j.jand.2014.12.011

Wing, R. R., Lang, W., Wadden, T. A., Safford, M., Knowler, W. C., Bertoni, A. G., . . . Wagenknecht, L. (2011). Benefits of modest weight loss in improving cardiovascular risk factors in overweight and obese individuals with type 2 diabetes. *Diabetes Care, 34*(7), 1481-1486. doi:10.2337/dc10-2415

Hungry for Connection

Barber, T. M., Hanson, P., Weickert, M. O., & Franks, S. (2019). Obesity and Polycystic Ovary Syndrome: Implications for Pathogenesis and Novel Management Strategies. *Clinical medicine insights. Reproductive health, 13*, 1179558119874042. https://doi.org/10.1177/1179558119874042

Kataoka, J., Tassone, E. C., Misso, M., Joham, A. E., Stener-Victorin, E., Teede, H., & Moran, L. J. (2017). Weight Management Interventions in Women with and without PCOS: A Systematic Review. *Nutrients, 9*(9), 996. https://doi.org/10.3390/nu9090996

Kessler, R. C., Berglund, P. A., Chiu, W. T., Deitz, A. C., Hudson, J. I., Shahly, V., Aguilar-Gaxiola, S., Alonso, J., Angermeyer, M. C., Benjet, C., Bruffaerts, R., de Girolamo, G., de Graaf, R., Maria Haro, J., Kovess-Masfety, V., O'Neill,

S., Posada-Villa, J., Sasu, C., Scott, K., Viana, M. C., …
Xavier, M. (2013). The prevalence and correlates of binge
eating disorder in the World Health Organization World
Mental Health Surveys. *Biological psychiatry, 73*(9), 904–914.
https://doi.org/10.1016/j.biopsych.2012.11.020

Lewer, M., Bauer, A., Hartmann, A. S., & Vocks, S. (2017).
Different Facets of Body Image Disturbance in Binge Eating
Disorder: A Review. *Nutrients, 9*(12), 1294. https://doi.
org/10.3390/nu9121294

Wekker, V., van Dammen, L., Koning, A., Heida, K. Y., Painter,
R. C., Limpens, J., Laven, J., Roeters van Lennep, J. E.,
Roseboom, T. J., & Hoek, A. (2020). Long-term cardiometabolic disease risk in women with PCOS: A systematic review
and meta-analysis. *Human reproduction update, 26*(6), 942–
960. https://doi.org/10.1093/humupd/dmaa029

Hungry for Control

Hsu, M. (2005). Neural systems responding to degrees of uncertainty in human decision-making. *Science, 310*(5754), 1680-
1683. doi:10.1126/science.1115327

Ryff, C. D. (1989). Happiness is everything, or is it?
Explorations on the meaning of psychological well-being.
Journal of Personality and Social Psychology, 57(6), 1069-1081.
doi:10.1037/0022-3514.57.6.1069

Ryff, C. D., & Keyes, C. L. (1995). The structure of psychological well-being revisited. *Journal of Personality and Social
Psychology, 69*(4), 719-727. doi:10.1037/0022-3514.69.4.719

Hungry for Sleep

CDC - data and statistics - sleep and sleep disorders. (2017, May 02). Retrieved April 07, 2021, from https://www.cdc.gov/sleep/data_statistics.html

Ford, D. E. (1989). Epidemiologic study of sleep disturbances and psychiatric disorders. *JAMA, 262*(11), 1479. doi:10.1001/jama.1989.03430110069030

Grandner, M. A., Seixas, A., Shetty, S., & Shenoy, S. (2016). Sleep Duration and Diabetes Risk: Population Trends and Potential Mechanisms. *Current diabetes reports, 16*(11), 106. https://doi.org/10.1007/s11892-016-0805-8

Hogenkamp, P. S., Nilsson, E., Nilsson, V. C., Chapman, C. D., Vogel, H., Lundberg, L. S., . . . Schiöth, H. B. (2013). Acute sleep deprivation increases portion size and affects food choice in young men. *Psychoneuroendocrinology, 38*(9), 1668-1674. doi:10.1016/j.psyneuen.2013.01.012

Ogilvie, R. P., & Patel, S. R. (2017). The epidemiology of sleep and obesity. *Sleep health, 3*(5), 383–388. https://doi.org/10.1016/j.sleh.2017.07.013

Patel, S. R., Malhotra, A., White, D. P., Gottlieb, D. J., & Hu, F. B. (2006). Association between reduced sleep and weight gain in women. *American journal of epidemiology, 164*(10), 947–954. https://doi.org/10.1093/aje/kwj280

Schmid, S.M., Hallschmid, M., Jauch Chara, K., Born, J. and Schultes, B. (2008), A single night of sleep deprivation increases ghrelin levels and feelings of hunger in normal weight healthy men. *Journal of Sleep Research, 17*: 331-334. https://doi.org/10.1111/j.1365-2869.2008.00662.x

Hungry to Nurture
Heise, A. M., & Wiessinger, D. (2011). Dysphoric milk ejection reflex: A case report. *International breastfeeding journal, 6*(1), 6. https://doi.org/10.1186/1746-4358-6-6

Nagasawa, M., Okabe, S., Mogi, K., & Kikusui, T. (2012). Oxytocin and mutual communication in mother-infant bonding. *Frontiers in Human Neuroscience, 6.* doi:10.3389/fnhum.2012.00031

Hungry to Grieve
Kübler-Ross, E. (1969). *On Death and Dying.* New York, NY: Collier Books/Macmillan Publishing.

Shear, M. K. (2015). Complicated grief. *New England Journal of Medicine, 372*(2), 153-160. doi:10.1056/nejmcp1315618

Simon, N. M. (2013). Treating complicated grief. *JAMA, 310*(4), 416. doi:10.1001/jama.2013.8614

Hungry for Legacy
Wrangham, R., & Conklin-Brittain, N. (2003). Cooking as a biological trait. *Comparative Biochemistry and Physiology Part A: Molecular & Integrative Physiology, 136*(1), 35-46. doi:10.1016/s1095-6433(03)00020-5

Hungry for Ease

Alcohol facts and statistics. (n.d.). Retrieved April 07,
2021, from https://www.niaaa.nih.gov/publications/
brochures-and-fact-sheets/alcohol-facts-and-statistics

Colrain, I. M., Nicholas, C. L., & Baker, F. C. (2014). Alcohol
and the sleeping brain. *Handbook of clinical neurology, 125,*
415–431. https://doi.org/10.1016/B978-0-444-62619-
6.00024-0Roehrs Alcohol Health Res World. 1995; 19(2):
130–135. Chen JAMA. 2011;306(17):1884-1890

Chen, W. Y., Rosner, B., Hankinson, S. E., Colditz, G. A.,
& Willett, W. C. (2011). Moderate alcohol consumption during adult life, drinking patterns, and breast
cancer risk. *JAMA, 306*(17), 1884–1890. https://doi.
org/10.1001/jama.2011.1590https://www.niaaa.nih.gov/
alcohols-effects-body

Grant, B. F., Chou, S. P., Saha, T. D., Pickering, R. P., Kerridge,
B. T., Ruan, W. J., . . . Hasin, D. S. (2017). Prevalence
of 12-Month alcohol use, high-risk drinking, and DSM-
IV alcohol use disorder in the United States, 2001-2002
to 2012-2013. *JAMA Psychiatry, 74*(9), 911. doi:10.1001/
jamapsychiatry.2017.2161

Otaka, M., Konishi, N., Odashima, M., Jin, M., Wada, I.,
Matsuhashi, T., . . . Watanabe, S. (2007). Effect of alcohol
consumption on Leptin level in serum, adipose tissue, and
gastric mucosa. *Digestive Diseases and Sciences, 52*(11), 3066-
3069. doi:10.1007/s10620-006-9635-x

Sheinbaum, H. (2020). *The dry challenge: How to lose the booze for dry January, sober October, and any other alcohol-free month.* New York, NY: Harper Design, an imprint of HarperCollins.

Valenzuela C. F. (1997). Alcohol and neurotransmitter interactions. *Alcohol health and research world, 21*(2), 144–148. Alcohol alert. (n.d.). Retrieved April 07, 2021, from https://pubs.niaaa.nih.gov/publications/arh25-2/101-109.htm

Hungry to Be Valued

Adult obesity prevalence maps. (2021, March 31). Retrieved April 07, 2021, from https://www.cdc.gov/obesity/data/prevalence-maps.html

Hari, J. (2018). *Lost connections: Uncovering the real causes of depression—and the unexpected solutions.* New York, NY: Bloomsbury.

Kivimäki, M., Ferrie, J. E., Brunner, E., Head, J., Shipley, M. J., Vahtera, J., & Marmot, M. G. (2005). Justice at work and reduced risk of coronary heart disease among employees. *Archives of Internal Medicine, 165*(19), 2245. doi:10.1001/archinte.165.19.2245

Marmot, M. (1993). Epidemiological approach to the explanation of social differentiation in Mortality: The Whitehall studies. *Sozial-und Präventivmedizin SPM, 38*(5), 271-279. doi:10.1007/bf01359588

Marmot, M., Stansfeld, S., Patel, C., North, F., Head, J., White, I., . . . Smith, G. (1991). Health inequalities among British civil servants: The Whitehall II study. *The Lancet, 337*(8754), 1387 1393. doi:10.1016/0140-6730(91)93008-k

Stansfeld, S. A. (2003). Social inequalities in depressive symptoms and physical functioning in the Whitehall II study: Exploring a common CAUSE EXPLANATION. *Journal of Epidemiology & Community Health, 57*(5), 361-367. doi:10.1136/jech.57.5.361

Hungry for Acceptance
Greendale, G. A., Sternfeld, B., Huang, M., Han, W., Karvonen-Gutierrez, C., Ruppert, K., Cauley, J. A., Finkelstein, J. S., Jiang, S. F., & Karlamangla, A. S. (2019). Changes in body composition and weight during the menopause transition. *JCI insight, 4*(5), e124865. https://doi.org/10.1172/jci.insight.124865

Makara-Studzińska, M. T., Kryś-Noszczyk, K. M., & Jakiel, G. (2014). Epidemiology of the symptoms of menopause— an intercontinental review. *Przeglad menopauzalny = Menopause review, 13*(3), 203–211. https://doi.org/10.5114/pm.2014.43827

Hungry for Power
Bertisch, S. M., Pollock, B. D., Mittleman, M. A., Buysse, D. J., Bazzano, L. A., Gottlieb, D. J., & Redline, S. (2018). Insomnia with objective short sleep duration and risk of incident cardiovascular disease and all-cause mortality: Sleep Heart Health Study. *Sleep, 41*(6), zsy047. https://doi.org/10.1093/sleep/zsy047

Brellenthin, A. G., Lanningham-Foster, L. M., Kohut, M. L., Li, Y., Church, T. S., Blair, S. N., & Lee, D. C. (2019). Comparison of the Cardiovascular Benefits of Resistance, Aerobic, and Combined Exercise (CardioRACE): Rationale, design, and methods. *American heart journal, 217,* 101–111. https://doi.org/10.1016/j.ahj.2019.08.008

De Lorgeril M, Salen P, Martin JL, Monjaud I, Delaye J, Mamelle N. Mediterranean diet, traditional risk factors, and the rate of cardiovascular complications after myocardial infarction: final report of the Lyon Diet Heart Study. Circulation. 1999 Feb 16;99(6):779-85. doi: 10.1161/01.cir.99.6.779. PMID: 9989963.

Dimsdale J. E. (2008). Psychological stress and cardiovascular disease. *Journal of the American College of Cardiology, 51*(13), 1237–1246. https://doi.org/10.1016/j.jacc.2007.12.024

Huang, T., Mariani, S., & Redline, S. (2020). Sleep Irregularity and Risk of Cardiovascular Events: The Multi-Ethnic Study of Atherosclerosis. *Journal of the American College of Cardiology, 75*(9), 991–999. https://doi.org/10.1016/j.jacc.2019.12.054

Lavie, C. J., Arena, R., Swift, D. L., Johannsen, N. M., Sui, X., Lee, D. C., Earnest, C. P., Church, T. S., O'Keefe, J. H., Milani, R. V., & Blair, S. N. (2015). Exercise and the cardiovascular system: clinical science and cardiovascular outcomes. *Circulation research, 117*(2), 207–219. https://doi.org/10.1161/CIRCRESAHA.117.305205

Hungry for Autonomy

Kivimäki, M., Ferrie, J. E., Brunner, E., Head, J., Shipley, M J , Vahtera, J., & Marmot, M. G. (2005). Justice at work and reduced risk of coronary heart disease among employees. *Archives of Internal Medicine, 165*(19), 2245. doi:10.1001/archinte.165.19.2245

Legault, L. (2016). The need for autonomy. *Encyclopedia of Personality and Individual Differences, 1-3.* doi:10.1007/978-3-319-28099-8_1120-1

Marmot, M. (1993). Epidemiological approach to the explanation of social differentiation in Mortality: The Whitehall studies. *Sozial-und Präventivmedizin SPM, 38*(5), 271-279. doi:10.1007/bf01359588

Marmot, M., Stansfeld, S., Patel, C., North, F., Head, J., White, I., . . . Smith, G. (1991). Health inequalities among British civil servants: The Whitehall II study. *The Lancet, 337*(8754), 1387-1393. doi:10.1016/0140-6736(91)93068-k

Moller, A. C., & Deci, E. L. (2010). Interpersonal control, dehumanization, and violence: A self-determination theory perspective. Group Processes & Intergroup Relations, 13, 41–53.

Patel, R., Bachu, R., Adikey, A., Malik, M., & Shah, M. (2018). Factors related to physician burnout and its consequences: A review. *Behavioral Sciences, 8*(11), 98. doi:10.3390/bs8110098

Ryan, R. M., & Deci, E. L. (2000). Self-determination theory and the facilitation of intrinsic motivation, social development, and well-being. American Psychologist, 55, 68–78

Hungry for Creativity
Cohen, G. D., Perlstein, S., Chapline, J., Kelly, J., Firth, K. M., & Simmens, S. (2006). The impact of Professionally conducted cultural programs on the physical health, mental health, and social functioning of older adults. *The Gerontologist, 46*(6), 726-734. doi:10.1093/geront/46.6.726

Flood, M., & Phillips, K. D. (2007). Creativity in older adults: A plethora of possibilities. *Issues in Mental Health Nursing, 28*(4), 389-411. doi:10.1080/01612840701252956

Michael Brady, E., & Sky, H. Z. (2003). Journal writing among older learners. *Educational Gerontology, 29*(2), 151-163. doi:10.1080/713844282

Hungry for Imagination
Burnette, J. L. (2010). Implicit theories of body weight: Entity beliefs can weigh you down. *Personality and Social Psychology Bulletin, 36*(3), 410-422. doi:10.1177/0146167209359768

Burnette, J. L., & Finkel, E. J. (2012). Buffering against weight gain following dieting setbacks: An implicit theory intervention. *Journal of Experimental Social Psychology, 48*(3), 721-725. doi:10.1016/j.jesp.2011.12.020

Crum, A. J., & Langer, E. J. (2007). Mind-set matters. *Psychological Science, 18*(2), 165-171. doi:10.1111/j.1467-9280.2007.01867.x

Dweck, C. S. (2016). *Mindset: The new psychology of success.* New York: Random House.

Ehrlinger, J., Burnette, J. L., Park, J., Harrold, M. L., & Orvidas, K. (2017). Incremental theories of weight and healthy eating behavior. *Journal of Applied Social Psychology, 47*(6), 320-330. doi:10.1111/jasp.12439

Kopelman, P. G. (2000). Obesity as a medical problem. *Nature, 404*(6778), 635-643. doi:10.1038/35007508

Stunkard, A. J., Harris, J. R., Pedersen, N. L., & McClearn, G. E. (1990). The body-mass index of twins who have been reared apart. *New England Journal of Medicine, 322*(21), 1483-1487. doi:10.1056/nejm199005243222102

Sorensen, T. I., Price, R. A., Stunkard, A. J., & Schulsinger, F. (1989). Genetics of obesity in adult adoptees and their biological siblings. *BMJ, 298*(6666), 87-90. doi:10.1136/bmj.298.6666.87

Hungry for Presence
Albertson, E. R., Neff, K. D., & Dill-Shackleford, K. E. (2014). Self-compassion and body dissatisfaction in women: A randomized controlled trial of a brief meditation intervention. *Mindfulness, 6*(3), 444-454. doi:10.1007/s12671-014-0277-3

Boccia, M., Piccardi, L., & Guariglia, P. (2015). The meditative mind: A comprehensive meta-analysis of mri studies. *BioMed Research International, 2015*, 1-11. doi:10.1155/2015/419808

Benson, H. (1976). *The relaxation response.* New York, NY: William Morrow.

Davidson, R. J., & Goleman, D. J. (1977). The role of attention in meditation and hypnosis: A psychobiological perspective on transformations of consciousness. *International Journal of Clinical and Experimental Hypnosis, 25*(4), 291-308. doi:10.1080/00207147708415986

Davidson, R. J., & Lutz, A. (2008). Buddha's brain: Neuroplasticity and Meditation [In THE SPOTLIGHT]. *IEEE Signal Processing Magazine, 25*(1), 176-174. doi:10.1109/msp.2008.4431873

Desbordes, G., Negi, L. T., Pace, T. W., Wallace, B. A., Raison, C. L., & Schwartz, E. L. (2012). Effects of mindful-attention and compassion meditation training on amygdala response to emotional stimuli in an ordinary, non-meditative state. *Frontiers in Human Neuroscience, 6.* doi:10.3389/fnhum.2012.00292

Hefter, R. (1977). *Very worried walrus.* New York: Holt, Rinehart and Winston.

Hungry for Meaning
Frankl, V. (2006). *Man's Search for Meaning.* Boston, MA: Beacon Press.

Epilogue: Just Hungry
Murphy, K., & Bloom, S. (2004). Gut hormones in the control of appetite. *Experimental Physiology, 89*(5), 507-516. doi:10.1113/expphysiol.2004.027789

Sanger, G. J., Hellström, P. M., & Näslund, E. (2011). The hungry Stomach: Physiology, disease, and drug development opportunities. *Frontiers in Pharmacology, 1.* doi:10.3389/fphar.2010.00145

Schellekens, H., Finger, B. C., Dinan, T. G., & Cryan, J. F. (2012). Ghrelin signalling and obesity: At the interface of stress, mood and food reward. *Pharmacology & Therapeutics, 135*(3), 316-326. doi:10.1016/j.pharmthera.2012.06.004

Zanchi, D., Depoorter, A., Egloff, L., Haller, S., Mählmann, L., Lang, U. E., . . . Borgwardt, S. (2017). The impact of gut hormones on the neural circuit of appetite and satiety: A systematic review. *Neuroscience & Biobehavioral Reviews, 80,* 457-475. doi:10.1016/j.neubiorev.2017.06.013

WHAT'S NEXT:

Join the Community:

Sign up for Dr. Adrienne's newsletter:
www.dradrienneyoudim.com
and for daily inspo on Instagram @dradrienneyoudim

ACKNOWLEDGMENTS

THIS BOOK BEGAN TO write itself long before I sat in front of my computer and there are countless people to acknowledge beyond those listed below. I hold you all in my heart.

To my father, who always said that I could do anything. Thank you for planting that seed in my consciousness; it has propelled me far and wide. I am grateful for your encouragement, your open ear, your phone calls on my drive to and from work and for our coffee dates. To my mother for teaching us unconditional kindness by example. I marvel at your ability to always be kind, do kind, and see kindness in others—your generosity is unparalleled. But what I treasure most is your mission to always fill our home with love. Whether we were living in our *mansion,* or that god-awful hotel, you normalized every experience, cooked with abandon, and brought people into our home and around our table for a shared experience that no one would ever forget. While I never will do it as well as you, I take so much pride in continuing this tradition in my own home and with my own children. Thank you for passing down this gift. To my brothers, Alex, and Allen, thank you for allowing me the privilege of the first born, for your trust and respect and for having my back. Alex, Suzie Salamander is just one of the many things I tormented you with. I am sorry! But in spite of the harassment, you must know how much I appreciated your companionship. You were not just my little brother but also my playmate. Allen, while you will always be the little baby boy with blue eyes, I am so proud of the man you have become. Thank you for holding down the fort; your efforts do not go unnoticed. I take comfort in you both and in knowing that we are in it together. To Helenie, my mother-in-law, thank you for the many school drop-offs and pickups and the hours you spent loving my jewels while I was away. Knowing you were there made working motherhood more tolerable, and I love you dearly. To Sabrina my identical cousin, we have shared scrambled eggs and twilight donuts, Puerto Vallarta and the Acropolis, Billy Joel, and Alanis, 5 am weight training and weekend walks on the beach. You have inspired my writing and corrected my grammar practically since diapers. God did not give me a sister, but she gave me the next best thing.

To my soulmate, remember when we used to fantasize about building it together? Step by step, bit by bit and piece by piece, we laid the pieces for this beautiful puzzle that is our lives. Thank you for being a true partner from the mundane daily tasks to monumental life changing endeavors. We have shared everything from dishes to diapers, *mommy* and me, school loans, cooking, pickups, play dates, the practice, renting and moving, renting and moving and renting and moving before we finally settled at home. We said we would do it and we did, and I am so damn proud of us.

To my three beautiful children, as they say in Farsi, *harchee begham cam goftam*. There is just no way to express how much joy I take in you three. Ellia, my *OG*, your arrival rocked my world. You were and continue to be the trailblazer in our home. I am so proud of the kind, mature, socially/environmentally conscience and morally just human that you are. I have no doubt that you will set this world on fire. To Cameron, my sweet-sandwiched boy. Your warm heart and infectious laugh light up the room and have ever since you were an infant. And while you dazzled us with your curly hair, brown eyes and abundant love, you cultivated your inner bad-ass—smart, enterprising and inventive, I am proud of you, Cam. And finally, Jolie, you are a fearless force to be reckoned with. You are bold, you are brave, and the purest and most delicious bundle of love. Thank you for your cuddles, your snuggles and your deep, deep empathy for us all. You melt my heart.

To my patients, thank you for trusting me with your stories and with yourselves; it is a privilege that I don't take for granted. To Melanie, you have been my cheerleader and my sounding board, throughout this soulful process. Thank you for keeping your promise to never blow sunshine up my ass, for drawing out my stories and doing so with such compassion and wisdom. Thank you, Will, for your gentle and diligent hand in polishing my work. Thank you to Lydia and the entire team for packaging my words so beautifully and finally thank you Marissa and team for believing in my message and helping me share it with the world.

To my students, thank you for giving me the privilege of your attention and eager minds. As they say in medicine, *see one, do one, teach one*; to participate in this tradition has been an immense honor. To the *many many* teachers and mentors over the years from my adored third grade teacher (Miss Luskey, thank you for showing me kindness when I needed it most) to Peggy, my *work-mom*, for your counsel and *kleenex* over the decade that spanned from me as a pregnant resident to my decision to flee the coop. I treasure your continued friendship. And finally, thank you to my most cherished teacher and confidant; you have educated my heart and left an indelible mark on my soul. I am forever grateful.

A note of gratitude to Multiversity 1440 for the serene refuge of your redwoods and to Alanis Morrissette, Alexander Elle and Dani Shapiro for the writing retreats you led in that beautiful space. Thank you to the many authors who have accompanied me over the past 2 years it has taken me to write this book: Anne Lamott, Elie Wiesel, Elizabeth Gilbert, Brene' Brown, Edith Eager, Krista Tippet, Antoine De Saint-Exupery, Steven Pressfield, Natalie Goldberg, Julia Cameron, Parker Palmer, Richard Rohr, Sharon Salzberg, Madeline Miller, Carol Dweck, Benjamin Hoff, Sue Monk Kidd, Stephen Bachelor, Johann Hari, Jerry Colonna, Ryan Holiday, Esther Perel, Don Miguel Ruiz, Mark Epstein, Daniel Siegel and Bessel Van Der Kolk, Pema Chodron, and Viktor Frankl. Your words nourished me to no end.

Finally, to those of you who have made it this far, to read my work and share in my thoughts, I sincerely thank you too.

With love and deep gratitude,

Dr. Adrienne